D0709056

PRAYER

90 DEVOTIONS FROM
OUR DAILY BREAD

COMPILED BY DAVE BRANON

Discovery House
from Our Daily Bread Ministries

Discovery House is affiliated with Our Daily Bread Ministries,
Grand Rapids, Michigan.

Requests for permission to quote from this book should be directed to:
Permissions Department, Discovery House
P.O. Box 3566, Grand Rapids, MI 49501,
or contact us by e-mail at permissionsdept@dhp.org.

ISBN: 978-1-62707-518-3

Printed in the United States of America

First printing in 2016

CONTENTS

FOREWORD

Think of those times in your life when you were brimming with excitement to talk to someone. Perhaps it was when you were a young adult and you had fallen in love. Each time you were able to talk to your special person, your heart beat faster and your smile grew wider.

Or maybe it was later in life when you knew you would be with a friend you hadn't seen in years. You had so much to catch up on, and you couldn't wait to start the conversation.

Do you feel some of that can't-wait-to-talk-to-Him excitement in your heart toward God?

He is the One who created a world of wonders and allowed us to live in it. The One who has existed in eternity past and will exist into eternity future. The One who knows us better than we know ourselves. The One who sent His perfect Son to earth to rescue us.

And we can talk to Him.

How do you view prayer? Does it sometimes seem to be less exciting than you know it should be? Do you wonder at times why you don't eagerly look forward to talking to God as much as you know you should?

Sometimes we simply need to reacquaint ourselves with the wonderful privilege we have to converse with our heavenly Father. That's what this book can help you to do. Through the ninety articles from *Our Daily Bread* writers, you can have your view of prayer refocused and your desire to talk with God reinvigorated. You'll be reintroduced to important Bible passages that remind you of the value and purpose of spending time in fellowship with the triune God.

Allow me to share one paragraph from the first article in the book—an article written by Keila Ochoa. Perhaps it best captures the essence and the excitement of prayer:

God desires a relationship with us. In the morning we can invite Him into our day, and then we can praise Him and ask Him for His help throughout the day. At other times we can treasure some time alone with Him and reflect on His faithfulness. As we spend time with God in prayer and in His Word, we grow in our relationship with Him and learn to become more and more like Him.

Doesn't that sound like what you want in your relationship with God? Dive into this collection about prayer. Perhaps as you read, you'll again sense that excitement and thrill that comes from being able to talk with the God of all creation.

—*Dave Branon*

CRUMBS OF TIME

Read: Daniel 6:10-23

Three times a day he got down on his knees and prayed, giving thanks to his God, just as he had done before. —DANIEL 6:10

A friend was coming to town. He is a very busy man and his schedule was tight, but after a difficult day in important meetings, he managed to see my family for half an hour for a late dinner. We enjoyed his visit, but I remember looking at my plate and thinking, "We only got the crumbs of his time."

Then I remembered how many times God gets the crumbs of my time—sometimes just the last minutes before I fall asleep.

Daniel was a busy man. He held a high government position in the ancient kingdom of Babylon, and I'm sure he had a full schedule. However, he had developed the habit of spending time with God—praying three times a day, praising God, and thanking Him. This routine helped him develop a strong faith that did not waver when he faced persecution (Daniel 6).

God desires a relationship with us. In the morning we can invite Him into our day, and then we can praise Him and ask Him for His help throughout the day. At other times we can treasure some time alone with Him and reflect on His faithfulness. As we spend time with God in prayer and in His Word, we grow in our relationship with Him and learn to become more and more like Him.

As time with God becomes a priority, we enjoy His company more and more.

—*Keila Ochoa*

Prayer Tip: **Get away as Jesus did (Luke 5:16).**

WHEN GOD IS QUIET

Read: 1 Kings 19:1-12

Then [Elijah] lay down under the bush and fell asleep. All at once an angel touched him and said, "Get up and eat." —1 KINGS 19:5

I love to take pictures of sunsets at Lake Michigan. Some are subtle shades of pastel. Others are bold strokes of bright color. Sometimes the sun sinks quietly behind the lake. Other times it goes down in what looks like a fiery explosion.

In pictures and in person, I prefer the latter. But both show the handiwork of God. When it comes to God's work in the world, my preferences are the same. I would rather see dramatic answers to prayer than ordinary provisions of daily bread. But both are the work of God.

Elijah may have had similar preferences. He had grown accustomed to being the center of God's grand displays of power. When he prayed, God showed up in dramatic ways—first in a miraculous victory over the prophets of Baal and then in the end to a long and devastating drought (1 Kings 18). But Elijah felt afraid and started to run. God sent an angel to feed him and strengthen him for his journey. After forty days he arrived in Horeb. God showed him that He was now communicating in a still small voice, not in flashy miracles (19:11–12).

If you're discouraged because God hasn't shown up in a blaze of glory, be encouraged anyway. Perhaps He's revealing himself with His quiet presence.

—Julie Ackerman Link

Prayer Tip: Be honest with God (1 John 1:9).

WAITING FOR AN ANSWER

Read: Psalm 9:1-10

Those who know your name trust in you, for you, LORD, have never forsaken those who seek you. —PSALM 9:10

When our daughter was fifteen, she ran away. She was gone more than three weeks. Those were the longest three weeks of our lives. We looked everywhere for her and sought help from law enforcement and friends. During those desperate days, my wife and I learned the importance of waiting on God in prayer. We had come to the end of our strength and resources. We had to rely on God.

It was on a Father's Day that we found her. We were in a restaurant parking lot, on our way to dinner, when the phone rang. A waitress at another restaurant had spotted her. Our daughter was only three blocks away. We soon had her home, safe and sound.

We have to wait on God when we pray. We may not know how or when He will answer, but we can put our hearts constantly before Him in prayer. Sometimes the answers to our prayers don't come when we would hope. Things may even go from bad to worse. But we have to keep persevering, keep believing, and keep asking.

Waiting is never easy, but the end result, whatever it is, will be worth it. David put it this way: "Those who know your name trust in you, for you, LORD, have never forsaken those who seek you" (Psalm 9:10).

Keep seeking. Keep trusting. Keep asking. Keep praying.

—James Banks

***

Prayer Tip: Forgive others before praying (Matthew 5:23-24).

SLEDDING AND PRAYING

Read: Mark 14:32-42

One of those days Jesus went out to a mountainside to pray, and spent the night praying to God. —LUKE 6:12

When the snow flies in Michigan, I like to get my grandkids, grab our plastic sleds, and go slipping and sliding down our backyard. We zoom down the hill for about ten seconds and then climb back up for more.

When I travel to Alaska with a bunch of teenagers, we also go sledding. We are hauled by bus nearly to the top of a mountain. We jump on our sleds and, for the next ten to twenty minutes (depending on levels of bravery), we slide at breakneck speeds down the mountain, holding on for dear life.

Ten seconds in my backyard or ten minutes down an Alaskan mountain. They're both called sledding, but there is clearly a difference.

I've been thinking about this in regard to prayer. Sometimes we do the "ten seconds in the backyard" kind of praying— a quick, spur-of-the-moment prayer or a short thanks before eating. At other times, we're drawn to "down the mountain" praying—extended, intense times that require concentration and passion in our relationship with Him. Both have their place and are vital to our lives.

Jesus prayed often, and sometimes for a long time (Luke 6:12; Mark 14:32–42). Either way, let us bring the desires of our heart to the God of the backyards and the mountains of our lives.

—*Dave Branon*

Prayer Tip: Set aside a place
to meet with God.

✘

MIRACLE RAIN

Read: 1 Kings 18:1, 41-45

I am God, and there is no other. —ISAIAH 46:9

Life is hard for the villagers who live on a hilly terrain in the Yunnan Province of China. Their main sources of food are corn and rice. But in May 2012 a severe drought hit the region and the crops withered. Everyone was worried, and many superstitious practices were carried out as the people attempted to end the drought. When nothing worked, people started blaming the five Christians in the village for offending the spirits of the ancestors.

These five believers gathered to pray. Before long, the sky darkened and thunder was heard. A heavy downpour started and lasted the whole afternoon and night. The crops were saved! While most of the villagers did not believe God sent the rain, others did and desired to find out more about Him and Jesus.

In 1 Kings 17 and 18 we read of a severe drought in Israel. But in this case, we are told, it was a result of God's judgment on His people (17:1). They had begun to worship Baal, the god of the Canaanites, believing that this deity could send the rain for their crops. Then God, through His prophet Elijah, showed that He is the one true God who determines when rain falls.

Our all-powerful God desires to hear our prayers and answer our pleas. And though we do not always understand His timing or His purposes, God always responds with His best for our lives.

—Poh Fang Chia

Prayer Tip: Set aside a specific time to pray.

GOD IS LISTENING

Read: Psalm 5

In the morning, LORD, you hear my voice; in the morning I lay my requests before you and wait expectantly. —PSALM 5:3

The day before Billy Graham's interview in 1982 on *The Today Show*, his director of public relations, Larry Ross, requested a private room for Graham to pray in before the interview. But when Mr. Graham arrived at the studio, his assistant informed Ross that Mr. Graham didn't need the room. He said, "Mr. Graham started praying when he got up this morning, he prayed while eating breakfast, he prayed on the way over in the car, and he'll probably be praying all the way through the interview." Ross later said, "That was a great lesson for me to learn as a young man."

Prayerfulness is not an event; it is a way of being in relationship with God. This kind of intimate relationship is developed when God's people view prayerfulness as a way of life. The Psalms encourage us to begin each day by lifting our voice to the Lord (Psalm 5:3); to fill our day with conversations with God (55:17); and in the face of accusations and slander, to give ourselves totally to prayer (109:4). We develop prayer as a way of life because we desire to be with God (42:1–4; 84:1–2; 130:5–6).

Prayer is our way of connecting with God in all of life's circumstances. God is always listening. We can talk to Him any time throughout the day.

—Marvin Williams

Prayer Tip: "We know that God does not listen to sinners. He listens to the godly person who does his will" (John 9:31).

ACCESS TO GOD

Read: 1 John 5:6-15

Let us then approach God's throne of grace with confidence, so that we may receive mercy and find grace to help us in our time of need.
—HEBREWS 4:16

Technology is a blessing in so many ways. Need a bit of information about a health problem? All you have to do is access the Internet where you instantaneously get a list of options to guide your search. Need to contact a friend? Just send a text, e-mail, tweet, or Facebook post. But technology can also be frustrating at times.

The other day I needed to access some information in my bank account and was asked a list of security questions. Unable to recall the exact answers, I was blocked from my own account. Or think of the times when an important conversation is cut off because of a dead cellphone battery, with no way to reconnect until you find a plug to recharge it.

All of this makes me delighted with the reality that when I need to access God in prayer, there are no security questions and no batteries required. I love the assurance that John gives when he says, "This is the confidence we have in approaching God: that if we ask anything according to his will, he hears us" (1 John 5:14).

God is always accessible, for He never slumbers nor sleeps! (Psalm 121:4). And thanks to His love for us, He is waiting and ready to listen.

—Joe Stowell

Prayer Tip: Keep track of prayer requests and answers.

THE SQUEAKY WHEEL

Read: Luke 18:1-8

The prayer of a righteous person is powerful and effective.
—JAMES 5:16

"The squeaky wheel gets the oil" is a popular proverb. As a child I rode my bicycle for long distances between home and school, and the squeaky sounds of the wheels drew my attention to the need to lubricate them.

In Luke 18, the widow's persistent request to the judge for justice against her adversary made her sound like a "squeaky wheel" until she got the result she needed. Luke explains that Jesus told this story to teach us the need to pray continually and not to give up, even if it appears that the answer to our prayer is delayed (vv.1–5).

God is certainly not an unjust judge who must be harassed before He responds to us. He is our loving Father, who cares about us and hears us when we cry to Him. Regular, persistent prayer draws us closer to Him. It may feel like we are a squeaky wheel if we keep going to Him, but the Lord welcomes our prayer and encourages us to approach Him with our cries. He hears us and will come to our aid in ways we may not expect.

As Jesus teaches in Matthew 6:5–8, constant prayer does not require long periods of "babbling." Rather, as we bring our needs before God "day and night" (Luke 18:7) and walk with the One who already knows our needs, we learn to trust God and wait patiently for His response.

—*Lawrence Darmani*

___

Prayer Tip: Sometimes pray short, one-sentence prayers.

FREE PRAYER

Read: Ephesians 6:10-20

And pray in the Spirit on all occasions with all kinds of prayers and requests. —EPHESIANS 6:18

A pastor was asked to call on a woman in a psychiatric hospital and pray for her. After his visit, he thought how good it would be for somebody to go there regularly and pray for the residents. The "somebody" turned out to be him. On a table in one of the wards, he put up a sign saying "Free Prayer." Later he recalled, "Suddenly I had fifteen people standing in line to get prayed for."

People often ask for our prayers, but do we faithfully pray for them? Many times we see others in great need but find it easier to discuss their plight with friends rather than to intercede for them. But people need and want our prayers.

Paul concluded his call to put on "the full armor of God" (Ephesians 6:13–17) by writing, "Pray in the Spirit on all occasions with all kinds of prayers and requests" (v. 18).

Oswald Chambers often referred to prayer as "the ministry of the interior" and said, "There is no snare, or any danger of infatuation or pride in intercession; it is a hidden ministry that brings forth fruit whereby the Father is glorified."

Faithful prayer—whether in public or private—is one of the greatest gifts we can give others.

—David McCasland

Prayer Tip: If you feel God is leading you to do this, have a day of fasting and prayer for people and situations that are heavy on your heart.

✕

IN JESUS'S NAME

Read: John 14:12-21

Until now you have not asked for anything in my name. Ask and you will receive, and your joy will be complete. —JOHN 16:24

One of my favorite collections of photos is of a family dinner. Preserved in an album are images of Dad, his sons and their wives, and his grandchildren in a time of thanksgiving and intercession.

Dad had suffered a series of strokes and was not as verbal as usual. But during that time of prayer, I heard him say with heartfelt conviction: "We pray in Jesus's name!" About a year later, Dad passed from this world into the presence of the One in whose name he placed such trust.

Jesus taught us to pray in His name. The night before He was crucified, He gave a promise to His disciples: "Until now you have not asked for anything in my name. Ask and you will receive, and your joy will be complete" (John 16:24). But the promise of asking in Jesus's name is not a blank check enabling us to get anything we want to fulfill our personal whims.

Earlier that evening, Jesus taught that He answers requests made in His name in order to bring glory to the Father (John 14:13). And later that night, Jesus himself prayed in anguish, "My Father, if it is possible, may this cup be taken from me. Yet not as I will, but as you will" (Matthew 26:39).

As we pray, we yield to God's wisdom, love, and sovereignty, and we confidently ask "in Jesus's name."

—Dennis Fisher

Prayer Tip: List general prayer needs: church, family, friends, government, schools.

IS HE LISTENING?

Read: Matthew 26:39-42; 27:45-46

About three in the afternoon Jesus cried out in a loud voice, "Eli, Eli, lema sabachthani?" (which means "My God, My God, why have you forsaken me?"). —MATTHEW 27:46

"Sometimes it feels as if God isn't listening to me." Those words, spoken by a woman who tried to stay strong in her walk with God while coping with an alcoholic husband, echo the heartcry of many believers. For many years, she asked God to change her husband. Yet it never happened.

What are we to think when we repeatedly ask God for something good—something that could easily glorify Him—but the answer doesn't come? Is He listening or not?

Let's look at the life of the Savior. In the garden of Gethsemane, He agonized for hours in prayer, pouring out His heart and pleading, "Let this cup pass from Me" (Matthew 26:39 NKJV). But the Father's answer was clearly "No." To provide salvation, God had to send Jesus to die on the cross. Even though Jesus felt as if His Father had forsaken Him, He prayed intensely and passionately because He trusted that God was listening.

When we pray, we may not see how God is working, or we may not understand how He will bring good through it all. So we have to trust Him. We relinquish our rights and let God do what is best.

We must leave the unknowable to the all-knowing One. He is listening and working things out His way.

—*Dave Branon*

Prayer Tip: Keep a list of missionary prayer needs handy.

FIRST RESPONSE

Read: James 5:13-16

Do not be anxious about anything, but in every situation, by prayer and petition, with thanksgiving, present your requests to God. And the peace of God, which transcends all understanding, will guard your hearts and your minds in Christ Jesus. —PHILIPPIANS 4:6–7

When my husband, Tom, was rushed to the hospital for emergency surgery, I began to call family members. My sister and her husband came right away to be with me, and we prayed as we waited. Tom's sister listened to my anxious voice on the phone and immediately said, "Cindy, can I pray with you?" When my pastor and his wife arrived, he too prayed for us (James 5:13–16).

Oswald Chambers wrote: "We tend to use prayer as a last resort, but God wants it to be our first line of defense. We pray when there's nothing else we can do, but God wants us to pray before we do anything at all."

At its root, prayer is simply a conversation with God, spoken in the expectation that God hears and answers. Prayer should not be a last resort. In His Word, God encourages us to engage Him in prayer (Philippians 4:6). We also have His promise that when "two or three gather" in His name, He will be "there . . . with them" (Matthew 18:20).

For those who have experienced the power of the Almighty, our first inclination often will be to cry out to Him. Nineteenth-century pastor Andrew Murray said, "Prayer opens the way for God himself to do His work in us and through us."

—Cindy Hess Kasper

Prayer Tip: "Enter his gates with thanksgiving and his courts with praise" (Psalm 100:4).

A POWERFUL LESSON

Read: Ephesians 1:15-21

Finally, brothers and sisters, whatever is true, whatever is noble, whatever is right, whatever is pure, whatever is lovely, whatever is admirable . . . think about such things. —PHILIPPIANS 4:8

In 1892, John Hyde boarded a ship in New York Harbor and set out for India. His goal was to proclaim the gospel to people who had not heard about Jesus. During the next 20 years he earned the nickname "Praying Hyde" because he often spent hours and even many days in prayer for the salvation of nonbelievers and the revival of Christ's followers.

On one occasion, Hyde was upset about the spiritual coldness of a pastor, so he began to pray, "O Father, you know how cold . . ." But it was as if a finger stopped his lips from uttering the man's name.

Hyde was horrified when he realized that he had judged the man harshly. He confessed his critical spirit and then determined not to focus on the shortcomings of others but to see them as individuals God loves. Hyde asked the Lord to show him things that were "of good report" (Philippians 4:8 NKJV) in the pastor's life, and he praised God for the man's virtues. Hyde learned later that during this exact time the pastor's spiritual life was revitalized.

Let's not be faultfinders—even in prayer. We can follow Paul's example of focusing on what God has done and what He can do in the lives of others (Ephesians 1:17–21). Instead of praying against people, let's pray for them.

—Joanie Yoder

Prayer Tip: Pray for your local fire and police departments.

A HEART FOR PRAYER

Read: Psalm 27:7-14

My heart says of you "Seek his face!" Your face, LORD, I will seek.
—PSALM 27:8

While traveling on an airplane with her four- and two-year-old daughters, a young mom worked at keeping them busy so they wouldn't disturb others. When the pilot's voice came over the intercom for an announcement, Catherine, the younger girl, paused from her activities and put her head down. When the pilot finished, she whispered, "Amen." Perhaps because there had been a recent natural disaster, she thought the pilot was praying.

Like that little girl, I want a heart that turns my thoughts toward prayer quickly. I think it would be fair to say that the psalmist David had that kind of heart. We get hints of that in Psalm 27 as he speaks of facing difficult foes (v. 2). He said, "Your face, LORD, I will seek" (v. 8). Some say that David was remembering the time he was fleeing from Saul (1 Samuel 21:10) or from his son Absalom (2 Samuel 15:13–14) when he wrote this psalm. Prayer and dependence on God were in the forefront of David's thinking, and he found Him to be his sanctuary (Psalm 27:4–5).

We need a sanctuary as well. Perhaps reading or praying this psalm and others could help us to develop that closeness to our Father-God. As God becomes our sanctuary, we'll more readily turn our hearts toward Him in prayer.

—*Anne Cetas*

Prayer Tip: Meditate on a passage of Scripture before praying.

✕

CONFIDENT ACCESS

Read: Hebrews 4:14-16

Let us then approach God's throne of grace with confidence, so that we may receive mercy and find grace to help us in our time of need.
—HEBREWS 4:16

Mont Saint-Michel is a tidal island located about a half-mile off the coast of Normandy, France. For centuries it has been the site of an abbey and a monastery that have attracted religious pilgrims. Until the construction of a causeway, it was notorious for its dangerous access that resulted in the death of some pilgrims. At low tide it is encompassed by sand banks, and at high tide it is surrounded by water. Accessing the island was a cause for fear.

Access to God for Old Testament Jews was also a cause for fear. When God thundered on Mount Sinai, the people feared approaching Him (Exodus 19:10–16). And when access to God was granted through the high priest, specific instructions had to be followed (Leviticus 16:1–34). Accidentally touching the ark of the covenant, which represented the holy presence of God, would result in death (see 2 Samuel 6:7–8).

But because of Jesus's death and resurrection, we can now approach God without fear. God's penalty for sin has been satisfied, and we are invited into God's presence: "Let us then approach God's throne of grace with confidence, so that we may receive mercy and find grace" (Hebrews 4:16).

Because of Jesus, we can come to God through prayer anywhere, anytime.

—*Dennis Fisher*

Prayer Tip: Don't forget to use prayer as an avenue of confession to God.

EFFECTIVE PRAYING

Read: Matthew 7:7-11

For everyone who asks receives; the one who seeks finds; and to the one who knocks, the door will be opened. —MATTHEW 7:8

A 12-year-old Cambodian boy named Lem Cheong began to question his family's religious beliefs. He had been taught that a person seeking guidance should go to a temple and shake a container of numbered bamboo slivers until one fell out. The priest then interpreted the meaning of the number. But this practice didn't satisfy Cheong's longing for clear answers, nor did it fill the void in his heart that only God could fill.

According to Harold Sala in his book *Touching God*, Cheong asked his uncle, a priest, if he had ever had a prayer answered. The man was shocked by the brashness of his nephew's question, but he admitted that he couldn't remember a single time one of his prayers had been answered.

Later Cheong asked a Christian if God had ever answered his prayers. The man recounted several instances. Cheong was so impressed that he accepted Jesus as his Savior that day. After that, prayer became a vital part of his life.

Jesus said, "Ask and it will be given to you; seek and you will find; knock and the door will be opened to you" (Matthew 7:7). Christian prayer is effective because God is the living and true God who hears and answers according to His will. And His will is always good.

—*Vernon Grounds*

Prayer Tip: Leave time in your prayer sessions to be quiet before the Lord and listen for His guidance.

ATTENDING TO OUR WORDS

Read: Psalm 66:10-20

But God has surely listened and has heard my prayer. —PSALM 66:19

A week after C. S. Lewis died in 1963, colleagues and friends gathered in the chapel of Magdalen College, Oxford, England, to pay tribute to the man whose writings had fanned the flames of faith and imagination in children and scholars alike.

During the memorial service, Lewis's close friend Austin Farrer noted that Lewis always sent a handwritten personal reply to every letter he received from readers all over the world. "His characteristic attitude to people in general was one of consideration and respect," Farrer said. "He paid you the compliment of attending to your words."

In that way, Lewis mirrored God's remarkable attention to what we say to Him in prayer. During a time of great difficulty, the writer of Psalm 66 cried out to God (vv. 10–14). Later, he praised the Lord for His help, saying, "God has surely listened and has heard my prayer" (v. 19).

When we pray, the Lord hears our words and knows our hearts. Truly we can say with the psalmist, "Praise be to God, who has not rejected my prayer or withheld his love from me!" (v. 20). Our prayers become the avenue to a deeper relationship with Him. At all times, even in our hours of deepest need, He attends to our words.

—*David McCasland*

Prayer Tip: Take a walk through your neighborhood and pray for your neighbors.

WAIT ON THE LORD

Read: Psalm 27

I waited patiently for the LORD; he turned to me and heard my cry.
—PSALM 40:1

With so many instantaneous forms of communication today, our impatience with hearing a reply from others is sometimes laughable. Someone I know sent an e-mail to his wife and then called her by cell phone because he couldn't wait for a reply!

Sometimes we feel that God has let us down because He does not provide an immediate answer to a prayer. Often our attitude becomes, "Answer me quickly, LORD; my spirit fails" (Psalm 143:7).

But waiting for the Lord can transform us into a people of growing faith. King David spent many years waiting to be crowned king and fleeing from Saul's wrath. David wrote, "Wait for the LORD; be strong and take heart and wait for the LORD" (Psalm 27:14). And in another psalm he encourages us with these words, "I waited patiently for the LORD; he turned to me and heard my cry. He . . . set my feet on a rock and gave me a firm place to stand" (40:1–2). David grew into "a man after [God's] own heart" by waiting on the Lord (Acts 13:22; see 1 Samuel 13:14).

When we become frustrated with God's apparent delay in answering our prayer, it is good to remember that He is interested in developing faith and perseverance in our character (James 1:2–4). Wait on the Lord!

—Dennis Fisher

Prayer Tip: List your government representatives—mayor, senators, congressmen, governor, president—and then pray for them.

PERSISTENT PRAYER

Read: Luke 18:1-8

Jesus told his disciples a parable to show them that they should always pray and not give up. —LUKE 18:1

A friend of mine has been a woman of prayer for many years. She has received countless answers from God, but sometimes she is disheartened because certain prayers for loved ones remain unanswered. Yet she keeps on praying, encouraged by the parable in Luke 18. This story features a widow who badgered a heartless judge for help and finally got it.

Jesus ended His parable with a question: If an unrighteous and disrespectful judge finally answers a pestering widow's pleas for help, shall not God answer His own children who cry to Him day and night? (vv. 7–8). The expected answer: "Of course He will!"

George Müller (1805–1898), pastor and orphanage director, was known for his faith and persistent prayer. Many times when he prayed for specific needs for his orphanage, God sent exactly what was required. Yet for more than 40 years he also prayed for the conversion of a friend and his friend's son. When Müller died, these men were still unconverted. God answered those prayers, however, in His own time. The friend was converted while attending Müller's funeral, and the son a week later!

Do you have a special burden or request? Keep on praying! Trust your loving heavenly Father to answer according to His wisdom and timing. God honors persistent prayer!

—*Joanie Yoder*

Prayer Tip: When you see troubling news or posts on Facebook, bow your head and pray for those involved.

)X(

CRYING OUT TO GOD

Read: Psalm 142

*Do not be anxious about anything, but in every situation, by prayer
and petition, with thanksgiving, present your requests to God.*
—PHILIPPIANS 4:6

After all these years, I still don't fully understand prayer. It's
something of a mystery to me. But one thing I know: When
we're in desperate need, prayer springs naturally from our lips
and from the deepest level of our hearts.

When we're frightened out of our wits, when we're pushed
beyond our limits, when we're pulled out of our comfort zones,
when our well-being is challenged and endangered, we reflex-
ively and involuntarily resort to prayer. "Help, Lord!" is our
natural cry.

Author Eugene Peterson wrote, "The language of prayer is
forged in the crucible of trouble. When we can't help ourselves
and call for help, when we don't like where we are and want
out, when we don't like who we are and want a change, we
use primal language, and this language becomes the root language of prayer."

Prayer begins in trouble, and it continues because we're
always in trouble at some level. It requires no special prepara-
tion, no precise vocabulary, no appropriate posture. It springs
from us in the face of necessity and, in time, becomes our
habitual response to every issue—good and bad—we face in
this life (Philippians 4:6). What a privilege it is to carry everything to God in prayer!

—*David Roper*

Prayer Tip: "Husbands, . . . be considerate as you live with your
wives, and treat them with respect . . . , so that nothing will hinder
your prayers" (1 Peter 3:7).

THERE'S POWER

Read: James 5:13-18

Therefore confess your sins to each other and pray for each other so that you may be healed. The prayer of a righteous person is powerful and effective.
—JAMES 5:16

When my sister found out she had cancer, I asked my friends to pray. When she had surgery, we prayed that the surgeon would be able to remove all of the cancer and that she wouldn't have to undergo chemotherapy or radiation. And God answered yes! When I reported the news, one friend remarked, "I'm so glad there's power in prayer." I responded, "I'm thankful that God answered with a yes this time."

James says that "the prayer of a righteous man is powerful and effective" (5:16). But does "powerful" and "effective" mean the harder we pray, or the more people we ask to pray, the more likely God is to answer with a yes? I've had enough "no" and "wait" answers to wonder about that.

Prayer is powerful, but it's such a mystery. We're taught to have faith, to ask earnestly and boldly, to persevere, to be surrendered to His will. Yet God answers in His wisdom, and His answers are best. I'm just thankful that God wants to hear our hearts and that, no matter the answer, He is still good.

I like Ole Hallesby's words: "Prayer and helplessness are inseparable. Only those who are helpless can truly pray. . . . Your helplessness is your best prayer." We can do helplessness quite well.

—*Anne Cetas*

Prayer Tip: Write out a prayer that focuses on an attribute of God.

PANIC OR PRAY?

Read: 2 Chronicles 14:1-11

Then Asa called to the LORD his God and said, "LORD, there is no one like you to help the powerless against the mighty. Help us, LORD our God.
—2 CHRONICLES 14:11

An 85-year-old woman, all alone in a convent, got trapped inside an elevator for four nights and three days. Fortunately, she had a jar of water, some celery sticks, and a few cough drops. After she tried unsuccessfully to open the elevator doors or get a cell phone signal, she decided to turn to God in prayer. "It was either panic or pray," she later told CNN. In her distress, she relied on God and waited till she was rescued.

Asa was also faced with the options of panic or pray (2 Chronicles 14). He was attacked by an Ethiopian army of a million men. But as he faced this huge fighting force, instead of relying on military strategy or cowering in dread, he turned to the Lord in urgent prayer. In a powerful and humble prayer, Asa confessed his total dependence on Him, asked for help, and appealed to the Lord to protect His own name: "Help us, LORD our God, for we rely on you, and in your name we have come against this vast army" (v. 11). The Lord responded to Asa's prayer, and he won the victory over the Ethiopian army.

When we are faced with tight spots, meager resources, a vast army of problems, or seemingly dead-end solutions, let's not panic. Instead, turn to God, who fights for His people and gives them victory.

—*Marvin Williams*

Prayer Tip: Sometimes, instead of coming to God with requests, spend time praising Him.

TWO-WAY COMMUNICATION

Read: Psalm 119:17-24

Your statutes are my delight; they are my counselors. —PSALM 119:24

Have you ever been stuck in a conversation with someone who talks only about himself? To be polite, you strike up a dialogue by asking questions. The other person proceeds to talk endlessly about himself, and he never once asks you anything. It is all about that person—and nothing about you.

Imagine what it must be like for our heavenly Father to listen to our prayers during our devotional time. We may have read a portion of His Word, but then in prayer we swiftly shift focus exclusively to our needs. We ask for help in solving a problem, providing for a financial need, or healing a physical ailment. But the passage we've just read doesn't even enter into our prayers. What God has just said to us goes largely unacknowledged.

Apparently the writer of Psalm 119 did not have this perspective. Instead, he sought God's help in understanding the Word: "Open my eyes," he said, "that I may see wonderful things in your law" (v. 18). And as he prayed he expressed how he treasured God's Word, calling it his "delight" (v. 24).

Let's develop a discipline of praying our response to the Word. It just might transform our devotional time. Bible reading and prayer should reflect a two-way communication.

—Dennis Fisher

Prayer Tip: Use a desk calendar to list your concerns day-by-day.

SURROUNDED BY PRAYER

Read: Romans 15:22-33

I urge you, brothers and sisters, . . . join me in my struggle
by praying to God for me. —ROMANS 15:30

My friend Melissa's 9-year-old daughter Sydnie was in the hospital for chemotherapy and a bone marrow transplant when I had a dream about her. I dreamed she was staying in a central room at the hospital with her parents. Surrounding her room was a block of other rooms where family and friends were staying and continually praying for her during her times of treatment.

In real life, Sydnie wasn't physically surrounded by family and friends in adjacent rooms. But spiritually speaking, she was and is surrounded by prayer and love.

The apostle Paul seemed to have a desire to be surrounded by prayer. In most of his letters to churches, he requested to be remembered in prayer to the Lord (2 Corinthians 1:11; Ephesians 6:18–20; Colossian 4:2–4; Philemon 1:22). To the believers in Rome, he wrote, "I urge you, brothers and sisters, . . . to join me in my struggle by praying to God for me" (Romans 15:30). He knew that he could not be effective in his service for God without His power.

The Bible tells us that Jesus also prays for us (John 17:20; Hebrews 7:25), as does the Holy Spirit, whose prayers are according to the will of God (Romans 8:27). What a comfort to be surrounded by prayer!

—*Anne Cetas*

Prayer Tip: Pray through the Psalms.

)(

CORNERED

Read: Luke 6:27-36

Bless those who curse you, pray for those who mistreat you.
—LUKE 6:28

One Sunday morning, D. L. Moody entered a house in Chicago to escort some children to Sunday school. During his visit, three men backed him into a corner and threatened him. "Look here," Moody said. "Give a fellow a chance to say his prayers, won't you?" The men actually allowed him to call out to God, and Moody prayed for them so earnestly that they left the room.

Had I been in Moody's situation, I might have called for help or looked for the back door. I'm not sure I would have acted on Jesus's command to His followers: "Pray for those who mistreat you" (Luke 6:28).

Praying for the people who treat us with contempt is one way to "do good to those who hate [us]" (v. 27). Jesus explained that Christians get no credit for swapping acts of kindness with other "nice" people. He said, "Even sinners do that" (v. 33). However, blessing our persecutors (Romans 12:14) sets us apart from them and aligns us with the Most High, because God is kind even to wicked people (Luke 6:35).

Today, if you feel "cornered" by someone, seek safety if the situation calls for it, and follow Jesus's teaching: Pray for that person (Luke 23:34). Prayer is your best defense.

—*Jennifer Benson Schuldt*

Prayer Tip: Get a book of collected prayers, and see if you can use that to enhance your prayer life.

UNANSWERED

Read: Luke 18:1-8

*Summon your power, God; show us your strength, our God,
as you have done before.* —PSALM 68:28

One of my biggest struggles is unanswered prayer. Maybe you can relate. You ask God to rescue a friend from addiction, to grant salvation to a loved one, to heal a sick child, to mend a relationship. All these things you think must be God's will. For years you pray. But you hear nothing back from Him and you see no results.

You remind the Lord that He's powerful. That your request is a good thing. You plead. You wait. You doubt—maybe He doesn't hear you, or maybe He isn't so powerful after all. You quit asking—for days or months. You feel guilty about doubting. You remember that God wants you to take your needs to Him, and you tell Him your requests again.

We may sometimes feel we're like the persistent widow in Jesus's parable recorded in Luke 18. She keeps coming to the judge, badgering him and trying to wear him down so he'll give in. But we know that God is kinder and more powerful than the judge in the parable. We trust Him, for He is good and wise and sovereign. We remember that Jesus said we "should always pray and not give up" (v. 1).

So we ask, "Summon your power, God; show us your strength, our God, as you have done before" (Psalm 68:28). And then we trust Him . . . and wait.

—*Anne Cetas*

Prayer Tip: Check out this book of collected prayers: *Classic Christian Prayers* by Owen Collins.

IN PARTNERSHIP WITH GOD

Read: Matthew 6:5-15

Do not be like them, for your Father knows what you need before you ask him. —MATTHEW 6:8

A man had transformed an overgrown plot of ground into a beautiful garden and was showing a friend what he had accomplished. Pointing to a bed of flowers, he said, "Look at what I did here." His companion corrected him, "You mean, 'Look at what God and I did here.' " The gardener replied, "I guess you're right. But you should have seen the shape this plot was in when He was taking care of it by himself."

We chuckle at the man's reply, but it expresses a wonderful spiritual truth—we are co-workers with God. This applies to every area of life, including prayer. It answers a question that naturally comes to mind when we reflect on Jesus's statements in Matthew 6. He said we don't need to pray on and on with vain repetitions like the pagans, because our Father knows what we need before we ask (Matthew 6:7–8).

The question is, then, why pray? The answer is simple and comforting. God has graciously chosen to give us the privilege of being His partners in both the physical and spiritual areas of life. Through prayer we work with Him in defeating the powers of evil and in bringing about the fulfillment of His loving purposes in the world. Partners with God—what a privilege! What an incentive to pray!

—*Herb Vander Lugt*

Prayer Tip: Remember PUSH: Pray Until Something Happens.

YOU CAN ALWAYS PRAY

Read: Acts 12:1–16

*When hard pressed, I cried to the LORD; he brought me into
a spacious place.* —PSALM 118:5

The young mother called out to the missionary, "Come quick!
My baby is going to die." Gale Fields was in Papua (a province
in Indonesia) helping her husband, Phil, translate the Bible
into Orya, a tribal language. But they also provided medical
help whenever possible. Gale looked at the malaria-stricken
child and realized she didn't have the right medicine to help
the infant.

"I'm sorry," she told the mother, "I don't have any medicine
for babies this small." Gale paused, then said, "I could pray
for her though."

"Yes, anything to help my baby," answered the mother.

Gale prayed for the baby and then went home feeling helpless. After a little while, she again heard the mother cry out,
"Gale, come quick and see my baby!"

Expecting the worst, Gale went to the baby's side. This
time, though, she noticed improvement. The dangerous fever
was gone. Later, Gale would say, "No wonder the Orya Christians learned to pray. They know God answers."

The early Christians prayed for Peter to be released from
prison and then were "astonished" when God answered them
(Acts 12:16). We respond that way too, but we shouldn't be sur-
prised when God answers our prayers. Remember, His power
is great and His resources are endless.

—*Dave Branon*

Prayer Tip: If you have family members who have strayed from the
faith, get James Banks's book *Prayers for Prodigals*.

NEVER TOO BUSY

Read: Psalm 145:8-21

The LORD is near to all who call on him, to all who call on him in truth.
—PSALM 145:18

College students rent a house from my sister and her husband. One night, a thief attempted to break in. When the young woman living there called the police to tell them that a break-in was in progress, the operator responded in an unusual way: "You'll have to call back in the morning. We're just too busy right now." That response was very disturbing! The young woman had done the right thing by calling the police, but for some reason her plea for help was disregarded. That kind of indifference is upsetting.

Indifference never happens when we go to God in prayer. We may not always feel that God is listening, but He is. He cares, and He will respond. The Bible reminds us that we can take comfort in the fact that our God is deeply concerned with what concerns our hearts: "The LORD is near to all who call on him, to all who call on him in truth" (Psalm 145:18). When we call out to Him, we will never get a disinterested response.

Rather than distancing himself from us when we cry to Him, our heavenly Father draws close to us in our time of need. He is never too busy for His child's prayers—He hears us when we call.

—*Bill Crowder*

Prayer Tip: Go on a personal prayer retreat—if only for a few hours.

✕

MINDLESS PRAYER

Read: Joshua 1:1-9

No one will be able to stand against you all the days of your life. As I was with Moses, so I will be with you; I will never leave you nor forsake you.
—JOSHUA 1:5

Sometimes I am ashamed of my prayers. Too often I hear myself using familiar phrases that are more like mindless filler than thoughtful, intimate interaction. One phrase that annoys me, and that I think might offend God, is "Lord, be with me." In Scripture, God has already promised not to leave me.

God made this promise to Joshua just before he led the Israelites into the Promised Land (Joshua 1:5). The author of Hebrews later claimed it for all believers: "Never will I leave you; never will I forsake you" (13:5). In both cases, the context indicates that God's presence has to do with giving us the power to carry out His will, not our own will, which is generally what I have in mind in my prayers.

Perhaps a better prayer would be something like this: "Lord, thank you for your indwelling Spirit, who is willing and able to direct me in the ways you want me to go. May I not take you where you don't want to go. May I not enlist you to do my will but humbly submit to doing yours."

When we are doing God's will, He will be with us even without our asking. If we're not doing His will, we need to ask for His forgiveness, change our course, and follow Him.

—*Julie Ackerman Link*

Prayer Tip: Pray for those who don't know Jesus worldwide—that they would meet Him, perhaps even miraculously.

TIME TO PRAY?

Read: Psalm 70

Hasten, O God, to save me; come quickly, LORD, to help me.
—PSALM 70:1

One morning, when I was a young child, I was sitting in the kitchen, watching my mother prepare breakfast. Unexpectedly, the grease in the skillet in which she was frying bacon caught fire. Flames shot into the air and my mother ran to the pantry for some baking soda to throw on the blaze.

"Help!" I shouted. And then I added, "Oh, I wish it was time to pray!" "It's time to pray" must have been a frequent household expression, and I took it quite literally to mean we could pray only at certain times.

The time to pray, of course, is anytime—especially when we're in crisis. Fear, worry, anxiety, and care are the most common occasions for prayer. It is when we are desolate, forsaken, and stripped of every human resource that we naturally resort to prayer. We cry out with the words of David, "Come quickly, LORD, to help me" (Psalm 70:1).

John Cassian, a fifth-century theologian, wrote of this verse: "This is the terrified cry of someone who sees the snares of the enemy, the cry of someone besieged day and night and exclaiming that he cannot escape unless his Protector comes to the rescue."

May this be our simple prayer in every crisis and all day long: "Lord, help me!"

—*David Roper*

———

Prayer Tip: Pray over public spaces in your neighborhood, such as parks and schools.

GOD'S ANSWERS

Read: Daniel 9:20-27

While I was still in prayer, Gabriel, the man I had seen in the earlier vision, came to me in swift flight about the time of the evening sacrifice.
—DANIEL 9:21

Daniel poured out his heart to God (Daniel 9:3). He had read Jeremiah and rediscovered God's promise that Israel's captivity in Babylon would last 70 years. So, in an effort to represent his people before God, Daniel fasted and prayed. He pleaded with God not to delay in rescuing His people (v. 19).

When we pray, there are things we can know and other things we cannot. For instance, we have the assurance that God will hear our prayer if we know Him as our heavenly Father through faith in Jesus, and we know that His answer will come according to His will. But we don't know when the answer will come or what it will be.

For Daniel, the answer to his prayer came in miraculous fashion, and it came immediately. While he was praying, the angel Gabriel arrived to provide the answer. But the nature of the answer was as surprising as the quick reply. While Daniel asked God about "70 years," the answer was about a prophetic "70 weeks of years." Daniel asked God for an answer about the here and now, but God's answer had to do with events thousands of years into the future.

Focused as we are with our immediate situation, we may be shocked by God's answer. Yet we can know that the answer will be for His glory.

—*Dave Branon*

Prayer Tip: "Pray continually" (1 Thessalonians 5:17).

44

WHERE DO I START?

Read: Luke 11:1-10

I call on the LORD in my distress, and he answers me. —PSALM 120:1

Several years ago, I was driving down the freeway when my car died. I pulled over to the side of the road, got out of the car, and opened the hood. As I looked at the engine I thought, *A lot of good this does me. I know nothing about cars. I don't even know where to start!*

That's how we might sometimes feel about prayer: Where do I start? That's what the disciples wanted to know when they suggested to Jesus, "Teach us to pray" (Luke 11:1). The best place to look for instruction is in the example and teaching of Jesus. Two questions you may have are the following:

Where should we pray? Jesus prayed in the temple, in the wilderness (Luke 4), in quiet places (Matthew 14:22–23), in the garden of Gethsemane (Luke 22), and on the cross (Luke 23:34, 46). He prayed alone and with others. Look at His life, follow His example, and pray wherever you are.

What should we pray? In the Lord's Prayer, Jesus taught us to ask that God's name be honored and that His will be done on earth as it is in heaven. Ask Him for your daily provisions, for forgiveness of sin, and for deliverance from temptation and evil (Luke 11:2–4).

So if you're looking for a good place to start, follow the example of the Lord's Prayer.

—Anne Cetas

Prayer Tip: "Be joyful in hope, patient in affliction, faithful in prayer" (Romans 12:12).

ALWAYS THERE

Read: Psalm 55:16-23

Cast your cares on the Lord and he will sustain you. —PSALM 55:22

The radio engineers who work at Our Daily Bread Ministries were getting ready to broadcast a program via satellite. They had prepared everything, including the satellite link. But just as they were to begin uploading, the signal to the satellite was lost. Confused, the engineers labored to reconnect the link, but nothing worked. Then they got the word—the satellite was gone. Literally. The satellite had suddenly and surprisingly fallen from the sky. It was no longer there.

I suspect that sometimes when we pray, we think something similar has happened to God—that for some reason He isn't there. But the Bible offers us comfort with the assurance that God hasn't "fallen from the sky." He is always available to us. He hears and He cares.

In a time of desperation, David wrote, "Evening, morning and noon I cry out in distress, and he hears my voice" (Psalm 55:17). No matter when we call on God, He hears the cries of His children. That should encourage our hearts. What was David's response to having a God who hears prayer? "Cast your cares on the Lord and he will sustain you" (v. 22). Although God may not answer as we would like or when we would like, we know that at "evening, morning and noon" He is always there.

—Bill Crowder

Prayer Tip: Be yourself in prayer.
You don't have to sound like your pastor.

⚭

KEEPING TRACK OF PRAYERS

Read: Matthew 7:7-11

With this in mind, we constantly pray for you, that our God may make you worthy of his calling. —2 THESSALONIANS 1:11

Shortly before an elderly acquaintance died, I wrote an article about her, telling of her diligence in prayer. Despite Margaret Koster's age, she set an example of faithfulness in prayer—continuing to spend hours each day speaking with the Lord she loved. Now she's reaping the rewards of that faithfulness.

But there's another story about Margaret that needs to be told—a story of how seriously she took her prayer-life. When she was younger, Margaret would pray each day for missionaries she knew about. She also kept a journal of her prayers—complete with answers.

One time when one of "her" missionaries was home from his overseas ministry, Margaret approached him, showed him her journal, and said, "I have recorded every prayer request you made as a missionary. And I have put down every answer that I know of. But I also have some prayers for which I don't know the answers. You need to sit down with me and tell me how God answered those prayers so I can write them down."

Now that's taking prayer seriously! We learn from Margaret not only the importance of prayer but also the reality of God's answers. Remember, "If we ask anything according to his will, he hears us" (1 John 5:14).

—*Dave Branon*

Prayer Tip: Don't forget the persecuted church worldwide. Fellow Christians are being mistreated and tortured for their faith. Pray daily for them.

OUR DEMANDING SCHEDULES

Read: Mark 1:32-39

The whole town gathered at the door, and Jesus healed many
who had various diseases. —MARK 1:33–34

Is your life too busy? Business deadlines, productivity quotas, and shuttling children to lessons and sporting events can really fill up your schedule. It's easy to think, *If only I didn't have so many responsibilities, then I could walk in vital union with God.*

Yet C. S. Lewis wisely pointed out that no one was busier than Christ. "Our model is the Jesus . . . of the workshop, the roads, the crowds, the clamorous demands and surly oppositions, the lack of all peace and privacy, the interruptions. For this . . . is the Divine life operating under human conditions."

We read of Jesus in Capernaum: "That evening after sunset the people brought to Jesus all the sick and demon-possessed. The whole town gathered at the door, and Jesus healed many who had various diseases" (Mark 1:32–34). The next day Christ sought out a solitary place and prayed. There He received direction from His Father to pursue a demanding ministry in another place. Our Lord communed with His Father and depended on the Spirit to minister through Him.

Is your schedule demanding? Follow the example of Jesus and set aside a specific time for prayer. Then depend on God's power to help you meet each day's demands.

—*Dennis Fisher*

Prayer Tip: Put a Post-it note in your line of sight at work with requests you can pray about during the day.

TEXTING GOD

Read: Colossians 1:3-12

For this reason, since the day we heard about you, we have not stopped praying for you. —COLOSSIANS 1:9

An article in *The Washington Post* told about a fifteen-year-old girl who sent and received 6,473 cell phone text messages in a single month. She says about her constant communication with friends, "I would die without it." And she is not alone. Researchers say that US teens with cell phones average more than 2,200 text messages a month.

To me, this ongoing digital conversation offers a remarkable illustration of what prayer could and should be like for every follower of Christ. Paul seemed to be constantly in an attitude of prayer for others: "We have not stopped praying for you" (Colossians 1:9). "Pray in the Spirit on all occasions with all kinds of prayers and requests" (Ephesians 6:18). "Pray continually" (1 Thessalonians 5:17). But how can we possibly do that?

Missionary Frank Laubach described his habit of "shooting" prayers at people as he encountered them during the course of each day. In a sense, he was "texting" God on their behalf, staying in constant communication with the Father. Laubach believed that prayer is the mightiest force in the world, and said: "My part is to live in this hour in continuous inner conversation with God and in perfect responsiveness to His will."

Pray continually. Perhaps what Paul urged us to do can be done.

—David McCasland

Prayer Tip: Remember that prayer is not just personal but also corporate. Read James Banks's book *Praying Together* to learn more.

QUIET TIME WITH GOD

Read: Psalm 23

He makes me lie down in green pastures, he leads me beside quiet waters.
—PSALM 23:2

The word *connected* captures our contemporary experience of life. Many people rarely go anywhere without a cell phone, iPod, or laptop. We have become accessible 24 hours a day. Some psychologists see this craving to stay connected as an addiction. Yet a growing number of people are deliberately limiting their use of technology. Being a "tech-no" is their way of preserving times of quiet, while limiting the flow of information into their lives.

Many followers of Christ find that a daily time of Bible reading and prayer is essential in their walk of faith. This "quiet time" is a disconnection from external distractions in order to connect with God. The "green pastures" and "quiet waters" of Psalm 23:2 are more than an idyllic country scene. They speak of our communion with God whereby He restores our souls and leads us in His paths (v. 3).

All of us can make time to meet with God, but do we? In Robert Foster's booklet *7 Minutes with God*, he suggests a way to begin: Start with a brief prayer for guidance, then read the Bible for a few minutes, and close with a short time of prayer that includes adoration, confession, thanksgiving, and supplication for others. It's vital to take time today to connect with the Lord, who is our life.

—*David McCasland*

Prayer Tip: Create prayer cards for family members with specific needs.

BAD IDEA

Read: Hebrews 10:22-39

Let us draw near to God with a sincere heart and with the full assurance that faith brings. —HEBREWS 10:22

The former athlete had neglected his body for too long, so he began an exercise routine. The first day, he did several push-ups and went for a light jog. The next day, more push-ups, a few sit-ups, and a longer run. Day 3: exercises and a mile-and-a-half run. On Day 4, our ex-athlete in retraining woke up with a sore throat.

Then he did one more exercise: He jumped to the conclusion that exercising was a bad idea. If all he got out of his huffing and puffing was sickness, it wasn't for him.

Let's examine another scenario. A Christian, realizing he has neglected his relationship with God, begins a new spiritual routine of Bible-reading and prayer. But after just a few days, some problems arise in his life. What does he conclude? Like the ex-athlete, should he decide that his spiritual quest was a bad idea and that it didn't do any good? Certainly not.

We don't pray and read the Bible to get a perfect, trouble-free life. Pursuing God is not cause and effect. We do it because it draws us closer in our relationship with the One who is perfect. The pursuit of godliness will not exempt us from trouble (2 Timothy 3:12). But a life dedicated to loving and pursuing God (Hebrews 10:22) is always a good idea—no matter what happens.

—*Dave Branon*

Prayer Tip: Create a daily prayer plan:
Monday, thankfulness;
Tuesday, praise; etc.

Ж

PASCAL'S PRAYER

Read: Philippians 4:4-13

So whether you eat or drink or whatever you do, do it all for the glory of God. —1 CORINTHIANS 10:31

Blaise Pascal, the brilliant seventeenth-century intellectual, made significant contributions in the fields of science and mathematics. He established the groundwork for the development of mechanical calculators and modern hydraulic operations.

As a young man, Pascal had a profound encounter with Jesus Christ. This life-changing experience motivated him to refocus his study from science and math to theology.

Pascal wrote a remarkable prayer that can help each believer in facing the tasks of life. He prayed: "Lord, help me to do great things as though they were little, since I do them with Your power; and little things as though they were great, since I do them in Your name."

Pascal's supplication is profoundly scriptural. Paul said, "I can do all this through him who gives me strength" (Philippians 4:13) and admonishes us: "Whatever you do, do it all for the glory of God" (1 Corinthians 10:31). Pascal echoes these admonitions to depend on God for His power and to view every act as important, since it will reflect on His glory.

The next time you face a huge task, remember that God is your strength. And when you encounter a seemingly insignificant one, determine to do it with excellence to the glory of God.

—Dennis Fisher

Prayer Tip: Create a prayer prompter for yourself: perhaps a rubber band on your wrist. When you see it, you'll be reminded to pray.

AN OLD MAN'S PRAYER

Read: Daniel 9:3-19

So I turned to the Lord God and pleaded with him in prayer and petition, in fasting, and in sackcloth and ashes. —DANIEL 9:3

Have you heard the story about the 85-year-old man who was arrested for praying?

You probably have. That's the story of Daniel, an elderly Jewish resident in Babylon sentenced to death for faithfully talking to God (Daniel 6).

Although the prayer that sent Daniel to the lions' den is his most famous talk with God (6:11), it wasn't the only time we see him in prayer.

In Daniel 9, we read an example of how he prayed. Daniel had been reading in his scroll of Jeremiah that the captivity of his people would last 70 years, and the people were 67 years into the exile (Jeremiah 25:8–11). He was eager for it to end.

God had called His people to live righteously, but they weren't doing that. Daniel decided to live righteously despite their lack of faith. He began to pray that God would not delay the end of the captivity.

As he prayed, Daniel focused on worship and confession. His pattern of prayer gives us an important insight into talking to God. We are to recognize that God is "great and awesome" (Daniel 9:4) and that "we have sinned" (v. 15). In prayer, we praise and confess.

Let's follow Daniel's lead. To him, prayer was as vital as life itself.

—*Dave Branon*

Prayer Tip: Stick a prayer-prompting Post-it note on your dashboard as a reminder to pray for, not be angry with, other drivers on the road.

LOST PRAYERS

Read: Psalm 86:1-7

When I am in distress, I call to you, because you answer me.
—PSALM 86:7

The headline read: "Unanswered Prayers: Letters to God Found Dumped in Ocean."

The letters, three hundred in all sent to a New Jersey minister, had been tossed in the ocean, most of them unopened. The minister had died long before the letters were found. How they came to be floating in the surf off the New Jersey shore is a mystery.

The letters were addressed to the minister because he had promised to pray. Some of the letters asked for frivolous things; others were written by anguished spouses, children, or widows. They poured out their hearts to God, asking for help with relatives who were abusing drugs and alcohol or spouses who were cheating on them. One asked God for a husband and father to love her child. The reporter concluded that all were "unanswered prayers."

Not so! If those letter-writers cried out to God, He heard each one of them. Not one honest prayer is lost to His ears. "All my longings lie open before you, Lord," David wrote in the midst of a deep personal crisis, and "my sighing is not hidden from you" (Psalm 38:9). David understood that we can cast all our cares on the Lord, even if no one else prays for us. He confidently concluded, "When I am in distress, I call to you, because you answer me" (86:7).

—*David Roper*

Prayer Tip: Ask your youth pastor for the name of a teen who needs special prayer, and talk to God about him or her.

BREAD FOR THE COMING DAY

Read: Matthew 6:9-13

Give us today our daily bread. —MATTHEW 6:11

Not long ago, I traveled to the Democratic Republic of Congo to lead a Bible conference. I took in the beauty of the Nyungwe Forest and Ruzizi River, which separates Congo from Rwanda. I experienced the amazing hospitality of the Congolese people, and I was moved by their sincere faith in God's provision.

Because unemployment, poverty, and malnutrition are serious problems there, the people often don't know where their next meal will come from. So each time they sit down to eat, they thank God and ask Him to provide the next meal.

Their prayer sounds a lot like Jesus's prayer in Matthew 6:11, "Give us today our daily bread." The word *bread* refers to any food. The word *today* indicates provision that comes one day at a time.

Many first-century workers were paid one day at a time, so a few days' illness could spell tragedy. *Daily* could be translated "for the coming day." The prayer would read: "Give us today our bread for the coming day." It was an urgent prayer to those who lived from hand to mouth.

This prayer calls Jesus's followers everywhere to recognize that our ability to work and earn our food comes from God's hand.

—*Marvin Williams*

Prayer Tip: Get the book *The Valley of the Vision* (Arthur Bennett, editor) and learn from the Puritan tradition of prayer.

A SURPRISE ANSWER

Read: 1 John 3:16-23

We have confidence before God and receive from him anything we ask,
because we keep his commands and do what pleases him.
—1 JOHN 3:21–22

When Josh McDowell's mother died, he was not sure of her salvation. He became depressed. Was she a Christian or not? "Lord," he prayed, "somehow give me the answer so I can get back to normal. I've just got to know." It seemed like an impossible request.

Two days later, Josh drove out to the ocean and walked to the end of a pier to be alone. There sat an elderly woman in a lawn chair, fishing. "Where's your home originally?" she asked. "Michigan—Union City," Josh replied. "Nobody's heard of it. I tell people it's a suburb of—" "Battle Creek," interrupted the woman. "I had a cousin from there. Did you know the McDowell family?"

Stunned, Josh responded, "Yes, I'm Josh McDowell."

"I can't believe it," said the woman. "I'm a cousin to your mother." "Do you remember anything at all about my mother's spiritual life?" asked Josh. "Why sure—your mom and I were just girls—teenagers—when a tent revival came to town. We both went forward to accept Christ." "Praise God!" shouted Josh, startling the surrounding fishermen.

God delights to give us what we ask when it is in His will. Never underestimate His desire to respond to our prayers. A surprise may be just around the corner.

—*Dennis DeHaan*

Prayer Tip: Use an app such as PrayerMate.

✕

BUT PRAYER

Read: Acts 12:5-7

So Peter was kept in prison, but the church was earnestly praying to God for him. —ACTS 12:5

When I was a pastor, I often visited residents in rest homes. I'll never forget one dear elderly lady I met. She was blind and had been bedridden for seven years, yet she remained sweet and radiant. One day she told me about a dream she had. She was in a beautiful garden where the grass was a luxuriant carpet beneath her and the fragrance of flowers filled the air.

She dropped to her knees, entranced by the scene. As her thoughts were drawn heavenward, she felt the need to pray for her own pastor, for me, and for others. When she awakened, however, she discovered that she was still in her hospital bed. With a smile she said to me, "You know, Pastor, at first I was a bit disappointed. But in a sense the dream was true. This old bed has been a garden of prayer these seven years!" Prayer had made her room a holy place of meditation and blessing.

Prayer also made a difference when Peter was in prison (Acts 12). It isn't always easy to pray, for real intercession takes self-discipline. Many of us lapse into saying fine-sounding words without truly praying. God often drives us to our knees through the press of circumstances, where we are to "look to the LORD and his strength; seek his face always" (1 Chronicles 16:11).

—Herb Vander Lugt

Prayer Tip: "By prayer and petition, with thanksgiving, present your requests to God" (Philippians 4:6).

THE SONG OF MARY

Read: Luke 1:39-56

And Mary said, "My soul glorifies the Lord." —LUKE 1:46

Mary was troubled. She had just heard the words, "Greetings, you who are highly favored! The Lord is with you" (Luke 1:28). Comforting words, it would seem, but startling because they were spoken by an angel.

Mary was about to be presented with the most magnificent news ever, yet she was fearful. And when the angel told her she would have a baby, she exclaimed, "How will this be, . . . since I am a virgin?" (v. 34).

Those two facts about Mary—that she was troubled and that she questioned the angel—tell us she was a person like us, with normal concerns.

Yet after listening to the angel, Mary called herself "the Lord's servant," and she said, "May your word to me be fulfilled" (v. 38). She was a humble, godly servant, with a willingness to do God's will.

We see more of Mary's heart in her eloquent prayer, known as the Magnificat, the Song of Mary (vv. 46–55). Here she rejoiced in God's holiness (v. 49), His mercy (v. 50), His strength (vv. 51–52), His care for the hungry (v. 53), and His goodness to His people (vv. 54–55).

We can learn from Mary to trust God despite our concerns and fears, and to praise Him for His greatness. That's what the song of Mary is all about.

—Dave Branon

Prayer Tip: Study the Lord's Prayer. Let Jesus teach you to pray.

IN CONFERENCE

Read: Luke 11:1-13

One day Jesus was praying in a certain place. When he finished, one of his disciples said to him, "Lord, teach us to pray." —LUKE 11:1

The president of a large company wanted to talk to the factory's manager about an urgent matter. But the manager's secretary said, "He cannot be disturbed. He's in conference—as he is every day at this time."

"Tell him the president wants to see him," the man responded impatiently.

The secretary firmly replied, "I have strict orders, Sir, not to disturb him while he is in conference."

Angrily, the man brushed past the secretary and opened the door to the manager's office. After one quick look he backed out, gently closed the door, and said, "I'm sorry!" The president had found his manager on his knees in front of his open Bible.

The purpose of a daily devotional time is to stimulate regular, intimate meetings with the King of Kings. We need to seek new orders and instructions each day from the One who has planned our lives and provided for our needs.

Jesus himself spent regular time in prayer and inspired His disciples to pray (Luke 11:1). He gave them what we know as the Lord's Prayer and told them to keep asking, seeking, and knocking (vv. 9–10).

Have you spent time in conference with God today? It's never too late to start.

—*M. R. DeHaan*

Prayer Tip: Pray out loud at times—especially if you find your mind wandering when you pray.

A BOLD ENTRANCE

Read: Hebrews 4:14-16

Cast all your anxiety on him because he cares for you. —1 PETER 5:7

One morning, Scott Long and his wife had just awakened and were lying in bed when suddenly a young fellow entered their bedroom. He walked around the bed to Scott's side.

If the trespasser had been a total stranger, his entrance would've been criminal intrusion. If he had been a friend, his entrance would've been just plain obnoxious. But it was their toddler son who had entered their bedroom, jumped on the bed, and boldly said, "I want in the middle." Scott was struck with the beauty of a child's security in knowing he is wanted.

We are welcome in our heavenly Father's presence as well. Hebrews 4:16 tells us we can "approach God's throne of grace with confidence, so that we may receive mercy and find grace to help us in our time of need." We can approach Him confidently about anything—our needs and our desires—knowing that He cares for us (1 Peter 5:7).

Writer Phillips Brooks said, "If man is man and God is God, to live without prayer is not merely an awful thing; it is an infinitely foolish thing."

Let's not be foolish and ignore the help we can find in prayer to our Father. Instead, let's approach Him with the boldness of a child who knows he is loved and wanted by his father.

—*Anne Cetas*

Prayer Tip: Get E. M. Bounds's book *Power through Prayer.*

PRAYERFUL THINKING

Read: Psalm 8

What is mankind that you are mindful of them, human beings that you care for them? —PSALM 8:4

Augustine was one of the most brilliant Christian thinkers of all time. Interestingly, he did some of his most effective and intimate praying while engaged in deep thought. He was what might be called a "prayerful thinker." Often Augustine began a line of reasoning and then concluded it with a prayer. Here is a sample from *Confessions*, one of his works on theology:

"Too late came I to love You, O Beauty both ancient and ever new; too late came I to love You. . . . You called to me; yes, You even broke open my deafness. Your beams shined unto me and cast away my blindness."

These are not the dry musings of some pseudo-theologian or armchair philosopher. They are the thoughts of someone with a passionate prayer life.

Prayerful thinking is not unique to Augustine. David pondered the beauty of creation and felt compelled to worship his Creator: "When I consider your heavens, the work of your fingers, the moon and the stars, which you have set in place, what is mankind that you are mindful of them?" (Psalm 8:3–4).

As we walk life's journey, our deep thoughts and feelings and our praying can be interwoven. Seeing the beauty of nature or even solving a problem can be opportunities for prayerful thinking.

—*Dennis Fisher*

Prayer Tip: Remember the ACTS prompt: Adoration, Confession, Thanksgiving, Supplication.

✕

EQUAL ACCESS

Read: Psalm 145:14-21

Let us then approach God's throne of grace with confidence, so that we may receive mercy and find grace to help us in our time of need.
—HEBREWS 4:16

Pastor Stuart Silvester told me of a conversation he had with an acquaintance who frequently flew his small private plane in and out of Toronto Pearson International Airport. He asked the pilot if he ever encountered problems taking off and landing his small craft at an airport dominated by so many large jets. His friend responded, "My plane may be small, but I have the same rights, the same privileges, and the same access to that airport as anyone else—even the jumbo jets!"

Pastor Silvester then made this spiritual application: "It's the same with prayer, with the believer's approach to the throne of grace. No matter who we are or how small we are in comparison with others or how low our station in life, we take a back seat to no one. No one is given priority treatment."

In a world that offers preferential treatment to the wealthy, the famous, and the influential, it's encouraging to know that every child of God has equal access to the Father in heaven. The psalmist said, "The LORD is near to all who call on him, to all who call on him in truth" (Psalm 145:18).

With that assurance, we can "approach God's throne of grace with confidence" in prayer, knowing that our loving heavenly Father will never turn us away.

—*Richard DeHaan*

Prayer Tip: From time to time, write out your prayers ahead of time so you know exactly what you want to talk to God about.

JOB OPENING

Read: Romans 12:9-16

Be joyful in hope, patient in affliction, faithful in prayer.
—ROMANS 12:12

Several years ago, a job became available in the church my wife and I attended. Just over a week before Christmas that year, my mother-in-law, Lenore Tuttle, died at the age of 85. When she went home to be with Jesus, she left a void not only in our family but also in our church. We were without one of our most faithful prayer warriors.

At Mother Tuttle's funeral, the presiding pastor showed the congregation her prayer box. It contained dozens of prayer cards on which she had written the names of people she prayed for every day, including one that mentioned the pastor's gall bladder surgery. On top of that prayer box was this verse: "Without faith it is impossible to please him: for he that cometh to God must believe that he is, and that he is a rewarder of them that diligently seek him" (Hebrews 11:6 KJV). She was a true prayer warrior who diligently sought the Lord.

Each day, many older saints, who have continued steadfastly in prayer (Romans 12:12), leave this earth through death and move on to heaven. This creates a "job opening" for people who will commit themselves to praying faithfully. Many of these positions remain unfilled. Will you fill one of them?

—*Dave Branon*

Prayer Tip: As Lenore Tuttle did, create a prayer box in which to keep your requests.

WHOM SHALL I SEND?

Read: Isaiah 6:1-8

Then I heard the voice of the Lord saying, "Whom shall I send? And who will go for us?" —ISAIAH 6:8

As a young pastor, I served a fledgling congregation that included my parents. My father was very active in the church's "people ministries"—evangelism, hospital and nursing-home visitation, bus ministry, relief for the poor, and more. Although he had never been formally trained in ministry, Dad had a natural ability to connect with people who were in the midst of hard times. That was his passion—the downtrodden people who are often overlooked. In fact, on the day he died, my last conversation with him was about someone he had promised to call on. He was concerned that his promise be kept.

I believe that my father's service was one that followed the heart of Christ. Jesus looked out over the masses of the forgotten people of the world and felt compassion for them (Matthew 9:36–38). He commanded His followers to pray that the heavenly Father would send workers (like my dad) to reach those weighed down with the cares of life.

My father became the answer to those prayers in many hurting people's lives, and we can as well. When the prayer goes out for someone to represent Christ's love, may our heart respond: "Lord, here am I! Send me."

—*Bill Crowder*

Prayer Tip: Remember FROG: Fully Rely on God.

GOD IS GREAT, GOD IS GOOD

Read: Nahum 1:1-8

The LORD is slow to anger but great in power; . . . The LORD is good, a refuge in times of trouble. —NAHUM 1:3, 7

When we were children, my brother and I recited this prayer every night before supper: "God is great, God is good. Let us thank Him for this food." For years I spoke the words of this prayer without stopping to consider what life would be like if it were not true—if God were not both great and good.

Without His greatness maintaining order in the universe, the galaxies would be a junkyard of banged-up stars and planets. And without His goodness saying "enough" to every evil despot, the earth would be a playground ruled by the biggest bully.

That simple childhood prayer celebrates two profound attributes of God: His transcendence and His immanence. Transcendence means that His greatness is beyond our comprehension. Immanence describes His nearness to us. The greatness of our almighty God sends us to our knees in humility. But the goodness of God lifts us back to our feet in grateful, jubilant praise. The One who is above everything humbled himself and became one of us (Psalm 135:5; Philippians 2:8).

Thank God that He uses His greatness not to destroy us but to save us and that He uses His goodness not as a reason to reject us but as a way to reach us.

—*Julie Ackerman Link*

Prayer Tip: Remind yourself occasionally of Psalm 66:18: "If I had cherished sin in my heart, the Lord would not have listened."

DOING OUR PART

Read: 2 Kings 20:1-7

I have heard your prayer . . . I will heal you. On the third day from now you will go up to the temple of the LORD. —2 KINGS 20:5

A runner at a school track meet crossed the finish line just ahead of his nearest rival. A bystander, noticing that the winner's lips were moving during the last couple of laps, wondered what he was saying. So he asked him about it. "I was praying," the runner answered. Pointing to his feet, he said, "I was saying, 'You pick 'em up, Lord, and I'll put 'em down.'" That athlete prayed for God's help, but he also did what he could to answer his own prayer.

When we ask God for help, we must be willing to do whatever we can, using whatever means He gives. When Hezekiah heard that he was going to die, he prayed for a miracle, and God promised to extend his life fifteen years. Then Isaiah gave instructions to place a lump of figs on the troublesome boil (2 Kings 20:5–7). God did the healing, but He used human effort and natural means.

A couple of children were walking to school one morning when it suddenly dawned on them that unless they really hurried they were going to be late. One of them suggested that they stop and pray that they wouldn't be tardy. "No," the other replied, "let's pray while we run as fast as we can."

—*Richard DeHaan*

Prayer Tip: If you are a grandparent, check out Kay Swatkowski's book *A Grandmother's Prayers*.

)(

MORE THAN WISHING

Read: Matthew 6:5-15

Do not be like them, for your Father knows what you need before you ask him. —MATTHEW 6:8

As a child, C. S. Lewis enjoyed reading the books of E. Nesbit, especially *Five Children and It*. In this book, brothers and sisters on a summer holiday discover an ancient sand fairy who grants them one wish each day. But every wish brings the children more trouble than happiness because they can't foresee the results of getting everything they ask for.

The Bible tells us to make our requests known to God (Philippians 4:6). But prayer is much more than telling God what we want Him to do for us. When Jesus taught His disciples how to pray, He began by reminding them, "Your Father knows what you need before you ask him" (Matthew 6:8).

What we call the "Lord's Prayer" is more about living in a growing, trusting relationship with our heavenly Father than about getting what we want from Him. As we grow in faith, our prayers will become less of a wish list and more of an intimate conversation with the Lord.

Toward the end of his life, C. S. Lewis wrote, "If God had granted all the silly prayers I've made in my life, where should I be now?"

Prayer is placing ourselves in the presence of God to receive from Him what we really need.

—*David McCasland*

Prayer Tip: "Call to me and I will answer you and tell you great and unsearchable things you do not know" (Jeremiah 33:3).

PANIC PRAYERS

Read: Psalm 37:1-8

Commit your way to the LORD; trust in him and he will do this.
—PSALM 37:5

In her book *Beyond Our Selves*, Catherine Marshall wrote about learning to surrender her entire life to God through a "prayer of relinquishment." When she encountered situations she feared, she often panicked and exhibited a demanding spirit in prayer: "God, I must have thus and so." God seemed remote. But when she surrendered the dreaded situation to Him to do with it exactly as He pleased, fear left and peace returned. From that moment on, God began working things out.

In Psalm 37, David talked about both commitment and surrender: "Commit your way to the LORD," he said. "Trust in him" (v. 5). Committed believers are those who sincerely follow and serve the Lord, and it's appropriate to urge people to have greater commitment. But committing ourselves to God and trusting Him imply surrendering every area of our lives to His wise control, especially when fear and panic overtake us. The promised result of such wholehearted commitment and trust is that God will do what is best for us.

Instead of trying to quell your fears with panic prayers, surrender yourself to God through a prayer of relinquishment, and see what He will do.

—*Joanie Yoder*

Prayer Tip: If you have children, make sure they see you praying—not just at the dinner table and never for show. If it is not legitimate, they'll know.

OUR PRAYER AND GOD'S POWER

Read: James 5:13-20

Pray for each other so that you may be healed. The prayer of a righteous person is powerful and effective. —JAMES 5:16

When we pray for others, we become partners with God in His work of salvation, healing, comfort, and justice. God can accomplish those things without us, but in His plan He gives us the privilege of being involved with Him through prayer.

When we intercede for a grandson in trouble, a mother having surgery, a neighbor who needs Christ, or a pastor who needs strength, we are asking God to provide for that person what we can't. We are acting as go-betweens, asking God to direct His power in a specific direction.

In his classic book titled *Prayer*, Ole Hallesby described how it works: "This power is so rich and so mobile that all we have to do when we pray is point to the person or thing to which we desire to have [God's] power applied, and He, the Lord of this power, will direct the necessary power to the desired place."

This assumes, of course, that we are praying "according to [God's] will" (1 John 5:14). Prayer is not a magic wand for satisfying our own wishes, but it's an opportunity to work with the Lord in accomplishing His purposes.

James told us "the prayer of a righteous person is powerful and effective" (James 5:16). So let's humbly and earnestly pray for one another.

—*Dave Branon*

Prayer Tip: While waiting in line at the bank, at the grocery store, at a ballgame, pray that God will work in the lives of the people around you.

MORNING, NOON, AND NIGHT

Read: Psalm 55:16-23

As for me, I call to God, and the LORD saves me. —PSALM 55:16

In 2003, a powerful earthquake struck northern Algeria. TV news images showed distraught people searching the rubble for survivors, while others numbly visited hospitals and morgues to see if their loved ones were alive or dead. Families stood together weeping and crying out for help. Their burden of uncertainty and grief could be seen, heard, and felt.

If you've experienced an intense loss, you'll appreciate the words of David in Psalm 55, penned during a painful time in his life. Oppressed by the wicked, hated by his enemies, and betrayed by a friend, David spoke of the anxiety and anguish that threatened to crush his spirit: "Fear and trembling have beset me; horror has overwhelmed me" (v. 5).

But instead of caving in to fear, David poured out his heart to God: "As for me, I call to God, and the LORD saves me. Evening, morning and noon I cry out in distress, and he hears my voice" (vv. 16–17).

Prayer lifts our eyes from personal tragedy to the compassion of God. It enables us to cast our burdens on the Lord instead of breaking under their weight. When our hearts are filled with pain, it's good to call on God in prayer—morning, noon, and night.

—*David McCasland*

Prayer Tip: "When you pray, go into your room, close the door and pray to your Father" (Matthew 6:6). (This does not exclude public prayer; it suggests that enhanced personal prayer is important too.)

MOUNTAINS CAN MOVE!

Read: Mark 11:20-24

"Have faith in God," Jesus answered. —MARK 11:22

A familiar slogan about prayer is, "Prayer changes things." But prayer doesn't do this—God does. Some people think that prayer itself is the source of power, so they "try prayer," hoping "it will work" for them. In Mark 11, Jesus disclosed one of the secrets behind all true prayer: "Have faith in God." Not faith in faith, not faith in prayer, but "faith in God" (v. 22).

Jesus told His disciples they could command a mountain to be cast into the sea, and if they believed it would happen, it would. Jesus then gave them His meaning behind that astonishing promise. He said, "Whatever you ask for in prayer, believe that you have received it, and it will be yours" (v. 24). Jesus was speaking about answered prayer. We can ask and receive answers only if our asking is directed to God in faith and according to His will (1 John 5:14).

I've often wished I could move mountains by faith. Having once lived in Switzerland, I'd like God to move the Alps into my backyard in England. But He has done something much more important: He has removed mountains of worry, fear, and resentment from my heart and cast them into oblivion through my faith in Him. He is still in the mountain-moving business! Have faith in God and pray.

—*Joanie Yoder*

Prayer Tip: Remember PRAY:

Praise, Repent, Ask, Yield.

)(

KEEP ON ASKING

Read: Luke 11:1-13

Ask and it will be given to you; seek and you will find;
knock and the door will be opened to you. —LUKE 11:9

I heard a woman say that she never prayed more than once for anything. She didn't want to weary God with her repeated requests.

The Lord's teaching on prayer in Luke 11 contradicts this notion. He told a parable about a man who went to his friend's house at midnight and asked for some bread to feed his unexpected visitors. At first the friend refused, for he and his family were in bed. Finally he got up and gave him the bread—not out of friendship but because the caller was so persistent (vv. 5–10).

Jesus used this parable to contrast this reluctant friend with our generous heavenly Father. If an irritated neighbor will give in to his friend's persistence and grant his request, how much more readily will our heavenly Father give us all we need!

It's true that God, in His great wisdom, may sometimes delay His answers to prayer. It's also true that we must pray in harmony with the Scriptures and God's will. But Jesus moved beyond those facts to urge us to persist in prayer. He told us to ask, seek, and knock until the answer comes (v. 9).

So don't worry about wearying God. He will never tire of your persistent prayer!

—*Joanie Yoder*

Prayer Tip: Approach God confidently (Hebrews 4:16).

A SIGNIFICANT IMPACT

Read: Daniel 10

For our struggle is not against flesh and blood, but against the rulers, against the authorities, against the powers of this dark world and against the spiritual forces of evil in the heavenly realms. —EPHESIANS 6:12

John Wesley was convinced that the prayers of God's people rather than his preaching accounted for the thousands who came to Christ through his ministry. That's why he said, "God will do nothing except in answer to prayer." An overstatement? Yes. But the fact is, our praying is a powerful weapon in the war between God and Satan.

In today's Scripture reading, Daniel was so disturbed by a revelation about Israel's future that he could do nothing except fast and pray. Three weeks later a heavenly messenger appeared, saying that God had sent him when Daniel prayed, but that the prince of Persia had detained him (10:13). This "prince" was an evil spirit who sought to influence the rulers of Persia to oppose God's plan. He had detained God's messenger until the archangel Michael came to his aid.

A cosmic conflict between good and evil is continually being fought in the invisible spirit world. Paul reminded us that it involves Christians. He listed the spiritual armor and weaponry we need for these battles (Ephesians 6:13–17), and then he added this: "always keep on praying" (v. 18).

Our prayers can have a significant impact on the outcome of those spiritual battles. May we, therefore, faithfully pray as we fight the good fight (1 Timothy 1:18).

—Herb Vander Lugt

Prayer Tip: Pray in the power of the Holy Spirit (1 Thessalonians 5:19).

CARING PRAYER

Read: Romans 15:30-33

I urge you, brothers and sisters, by our Lord Jesus Christ and by the love of the Spirit, to join me in my struggle by praying to God for me.
—ROMANS 15:30

I recently received an e-mail from someone I didn't know. It was from a teenager who set a great example we all can learn from. His e-mail showed how much he believed in the power of prayer.

He told about a teenage girl in his hometown who had become pregnant outside of marriage. Her parents were threatening to force her to get an abortion. When the young man heard about it, he got on his computer and sent an e-mail to more than one hundred people, telling of the girl's predicament and saying over and over, "Please pray for this girl." His compassion for her was evident—as well as his faith in God to answer prayer.

This teenager could have spent time on his computer doing many other things: looking up information about cars, playing video games, posting cat videos. Instead, he took the time to compile all those e-mail addresses, and then he wrote a caring, heartfelt note. In Romans 15:30–33, the apostle Paul showed that he knew the value of concerted prayer—whether it's for ourselves or for someone else in need.

What a lesson! It reminds us to cling to the Lord in prayer, and it shows us an example of the compassion that leads us to team up with others in caring prayer.

—*Dave Branon*

Prayer Tip: Don't forget to follow up with God and thank Him for the answers to prayer He sends your way.

LIMITATION OR ADVANTAGE?

Read: 2 Corinthians 12:1-10

But [the Lord] said to me, "My grace is sufficient for you, for my power is made perfect in weakness." —2 CORINTHIANS 12:9

We've been taught that when we ask God for something through prayer, His answer may be *yes, no,* or *wait.* We're told that even *no* is an answer, though obviously not the one we may want. It certainly wasn't the answer Paul wanted when he begged God three times to remove what he called "a thorn in my flesh" (2 Corinthians 12:7–8).

Whatever Paul's thorn was, it weakened him. Because he wanted to be strong in his ministry, Paul asked God for deliverance. Although God didn't grant his request, He answered his prayer! He said to Paul, "My grace is sufficient for you, for my power is made perfect in weakness" (v. 9). The all-sufficient strength of Christ became Paul's new boast.

Author J. Oswald Sanders summarized Paul's attitude about his thorn like this: "At first he viewed it as a limiting handicap, but later he came to regard it as a heavenly advantage." Paul could therefore testify, "I delight in weaknesses, in insults, in hardships, in persecutions, in difficulties. For when I am weak, then I am strong" (v. 10).

Have you prayed for deliverance from something that weakens you, but deliverance hasn't come? Remember, God's grace is sufficient for you. He can transform your limitation into your "heavenly advantage."

—Joanie Yoder

Prayer Tip: Read prayers written by others, such as Oswald Chambers in Knocking at God's Door.

UNANSWERED PRAYERS

Read: Matthew 26:36-44

[Jesus] went away a second time and prayed, "My Father,
it if is not possible for this cup to be taken away unless I drink it,
may your will be done." —MATTHEW 26:42

Have you or a friend been afflicted with an illness for which there is no medical cure? Has God denied your repeated requests for healing? Has His refusal to say yes caused you to question His purpose?

An article by Carol Bradley tells us about the wisdom of Craig Satterlee, a seminary professor in Chicago. He has been legally blind since birth, with only twenty percent of normal vision. Does he complain, saying that God has not kept His promise to answer prayer? By no means! He believes wholeheartedly that God has given him something even better.

"I am whole," he testifies, "even though I am legally blind." If introduced as a believer in the power of prayer, he graciously explains, "I don't believe in the power of prayer. I believe in the power and presence of God, so I pray." He adds, "We know that God brings light out of darkness, life out of death, hope out of despair. That's what Scripture teaches us."

Prayer isn't the way to get God to do whatever we want. It's an expression of our trust in His power, wisdom, and grace. No matter what we ask God to do for us, we are to have the attitude of Jesus, who said, "Yet not as I will, but as you will" (Matthew 26:39).

—Vernon Grounds

Prayer Tip: "The Spirit helps us in our weakness. We do not know what we ought to pray for, but the Spirit himself intercedes for us through wordless groans" (Romans 8:26).

☒

WAITING . . .

Be joyful in hope, patient in affliction, faithful in prayer.
—ROMANS 12:12

Day after day for years Harry shared with the Lord his concern for his son-in-law John, who had turned away from God. But then Harry died. A few months later, John turned back to God. When his mother-in-law Marsha told him that Harry had been praying for him every day, John replied, "I waited too long." But Marsha joyfully shared: "The Lord is still answering the prayers Harry prayed during his earthly life."

Harry's story is an encouragement to us who pray and wait. He was "faithful in prayer" and waited patiently (Romans 12:12).

The author of Psalm 130 experienced waiting in prayer. He said, "I wait for the LORD, my whole being waits" (v. 5). He found hope in God because he knew that "with the LORD is unfailing love and with him is full redemption" (v. 7).

Author Samuel Enyia wrote about God's timing: "God does not depend on our time. Our time is chronological and linear but God . . . is timeless. He will act at the fullness of His time. Our prayer . . . may not necessarily rush God into action, but . . . places us before Him in fellowship."

What a privilege we have to fellowship with God in prayer and to wait for the answer in the fullness of His time.

—*Anne Cetas*

Prayer Tip: Write down little nudgings and promptings from the Holy Spirit. Ask for courage to carry through on those.

ALL DAY WITH GOD

Read: 1 Thessalonians 5:12-18

Pray continually. —1 THESSALONIANS 5:17

Brother Lawrence (1614–1691) felt intimately close to God as he humbly scrubbed pots and pans in the monastery kitchen. Certainly Brother Lawrence practiced specific times of devotional prayer. But what he found more life-transforming was prayer during the workday. In his devotional classic *Practicing the Presence of God*, he says, "It is a great delusion to think our times of prayer ought to differ from other times. We are as strictly obliged to cleave to God by action in the time of action as by prayer in the season of prayer." In short, he advocated that we "pray continually" (1 Thessalonians 5:17).

That's a helpful reminder because sometimes we tend to compartmentalize our lives. Perhaps we pray only during church worship, small-group Bible study, family devotions, and personal quiet times. But what about during our workday? To pray on the job does not mean we have to fall to our knees with clasped hands and pray aloud. But it does mean that work decisions and relationships can be brought to God throughout the day.

Wherever we are and whatever we're doing, God wants to be a part of it. When prayer enters every aspect of our lives, who knows what God might do for His glory!

—*Dennis Fisher*

Prayer Tip: "The LORD is near to all who call on him, to all who call on him in truth" (Psalm 145:18).

HOW LONG?

Read: Psalm 13

How long, LORD? Will you forget me forever? How long will you hide your face from me? —PSALM 13:1

My friends Bob and Delores understand what it means to wait for answers—answers that never seem to come. When their son Jason and future daughter-in-law Lindsay were murdered, a national manhunt was undertaken to find the killer and bring him to justice. After several years of prayer and pursuit, there were still no tangible answers to the painful questions the two hurting families wrestled with. There was only silence.

In such times, we are vulnerable to wrong assumptions and conclusions about life, about God, and about prayer. In Psalm 13, David wrestled with the problem of unanswered prayer. He questioned why the world was so dangerous and pleaded for answers from God.

It's a hard psalm that David sang, and it seems to be one of frustration. Yet, in the end, his doubts and fears turned to trust. Why? Because the circumstances of our struggles cannot diminish the character of God and His care for His children. In verse 5, David turned a corner. From his heart he prayed, "But I trust in your unfailing love; my heart rejoices in your salvation."

In the pain and struggle of living without answers, we can always find comfort in our heavenly Father.

—*Bill Crowder*

Prayer Tip: "Watch and pray so that you will not fall into temptation. The spirit is willing, but the flesh is weak" (Matthew 26:41).

FIVE-FINGER PRAYERS

Read: James 5:13–18

Therefore confess your sins to each other and pray for each other.
—JAMES 5:16

Prayer is a conversation with God, not a formula. Yet sometimes we might need to use a "method" to freshen up our prayer time. We can pray the Psalms or other Scriptures (such as the Lord's Prayer), or use the ACTS method (Adoration, Confession, Thanksgiving, and Supplication). I recently came across this "Five-Finger Prayer" to use as a guide when praying for others:

- When you fold your hands, the thumb is nearest you. So begin by praying for those closest to you—your loved ones (Philippians 1:3–5).
- The index finger is the pointer. Pray for those who teach—Bible teachers and preachers, and those who teach children (1 Thessalonians 5:25).
- The next finger is the tallest. It reminds you to pray for those in authority over you—national and local leaders and your supervisor at work (1 Timothy 2:1–2).
- The fourth finger is usually the weakest. Pray for those who are in trouble or who are suffering (James 5:13–16).
- Then comes your little finger. It reminds you of your smallness in relation to God's greatness. Ask Him to supply your needs (Philippians 4:6, 19).

—*Anne Cetas*

Prayer Tip: Always incorporate your church in your prayers—pray for and with the people.

WHEN IT'S HARD TO PRAY

Read: Romans 8:26-27

Before a word is on my tongue you, LORD, know it completely.
—PSALM 139:4

The Bible tells us that God knows our every thought and every word on our tongue (Psalm 139:1–4). And when we don't know what to pray for, the Holy Spirit "intercedes for us through wordless groans" (Romans 8:26).

These biblical truths assure us that we can have communication with God even without a word being spoken, because He knows the intentions and desires of our heart. What a comfort when we are perplexed or in deep distress! We don't have to worry if we can't find the words to express our thoughts and feelings. We don't have to feel embarrassed if sometimes our sentences break off half-finished. God knows what we were going to say. We don't have to feel guilty if our thoughts wander and we have to struggle to keep our minds focused on the Lord.

And for that matter, we don't have to worry about a proper posture in prayer. If we are elderly or arthritic and can't kneel, that's okay. What God cares about is the posture of our heart.

What a wonderful God! No matter how much you falter and stumble in your praying, He hears you. His heart of infinite love responds to the needs and emotions of your own inarticulate heart. So keep on praying!

—*Vernon Grounds*

Prayer Tip: Experiment with different prayer postures: on your knees, at a desk, standing and walking, hands folded, or not.

X

WORRIER OR WARRIOR?

Read: Ephesians 3:14-21

Now to him who is able to do immeasurably more than all we ask
or imagine, according to his power that is at work within us.
—EPHESIANS 3:20

A missionary wrote a newsletter to thank his supporters for being "prayer warriors." Because of a typing error, though, he called them "prayer *worriers*." For some of us, that might be a good description.

In his book *Growing Your Soul*, Neil Wiseman writes, "Prayer must be more than a kind of restatement of fretting worries or a mulling over of problems. Our petitions must move beyond gloomy desperation, which deals mostly with calamity and despair."

During an anxious time in my life, I became a "prayer worrier." I would beg, "Lord, please keep my neighbor from causing me problems tomorrow." Or, "Father, don't let that ornery person spread gossip about me."

But then the Lord taught me to pray *for* people, rather than *against* them. I began to say, "Lord, bless and encourage my neighbor, and help him to sense your love." Then I watched to see what God would do. The Lord's amazing answers not only helped others but also helped to cure my own anxiety!

Paul was no "prayer worrier." He prayed for God's people that they might know the strength, love, and fullness of God, who is able to do far more than we can ask or even think (Ephesians 3:14–21). Such confidence made Paul a true "prayer warrior." Are your prayers like that?

—*Joanie Yoder*

___

Prayer Tip: If you have children, pray over them using James Banks's book *Prayers for Your Children*.

PRAYING WITH BOLDNESS

Read: Psalm 6

*In [Christ] and through faith in him we may approach God
with freedom and confidence.* —EPHESIANS 3:12

Have you ever found it tough to pray? That can happen when
we're reluctant to tell God how we're really feeling. We might
abruptly stop in mid-sentence, fearful of being disrespectful of
our heavenly Father.

A trip through the book of Psalms can help us pray more
openly. There we can overhear David's conversations with God
and realize that he was not afraid to be completely open and
honest with the Lord. David cried out: "LORD, do not rebuke
me in your anger" (Psalm 6:1). "Have mercy on me, LORD, for
I am faint" (6:2). "Why, LORD, do you stand far off?" (10:1).
"Do not turn a deaf ear to me" (28:1). "Contend, LORD, with
those who contend with me" (35:1). "Hear my prayer, O God"
(54:2). "My thoughts trouble me and I am distraught" (55:2).

Think about David's approach. He was saying to God:
"Help me!" "Listen to me!" "Don't be mad at me!" "Where
are you?" David boldly went to God and told Him what was
on his mind. Yes, God expects us to come to Him with a clean
heart, and we need to approach Him with reverence—but we
don't have to be afraid to tell God what we're thinking and
feeling.

Next time you talk with your heavenly Father—tell it
straight. He'll listen, and He'll understand.

—*Dave Branon*

Prayer Tip: "Devote yourselves to prayer, being watchful and
thankful" (Colossians 4:2).

ALWAYS ON CALL

Read: Psalm 34:1-18

This poor man called, and the LORD heard him; he saved him out of all his troubles. —PSALM 34:6

If you're frustrated with the health care system and would like a personal physician who is always on call, you can have one—for a price. Two Seattle doctors are charging wealthy patients $20,000 a year for primary healthcare. They make house calls, give personal, unhurried treatment, and say the service they provide is like other perks available to people with money. Whatever we think of the medical ethics involved, it's a level of care most of us would like to have if we could afford it.

There's another type of "on-call" relationship that cannot be purchased. In fact, it's available only to those who consider themselves poor and needy. I'm speaking of God's never-failing response to His children who cry out to Him for help.

David said, "I sought the LORD, and he answered me; he delivered me from all my fears" (Psalm 34:4). He also said, "This poor man called, and the LORD heard him; he saved him out of all his troubles" (v. 6).

Jesus has been called "the Great Physician." He is not "on demand" to do as we ask, but He is always "on call" to hear our prayers and provide the deliverance we need. What an encouragement! "The eyes of the LORD are on the righteous, and his ears are attentive to their cry" (v. 15).

—*David McCasland*

___

Prayer Tip: Journal your prayer requests and answers.

PRAYING AND WORKING

Read: Matthew 9:35–10:1

Evening, morning and noon I cry out in distress, and he hears my voice.
—PSALM 55:17

While driving through a small town in Pennsylvania, I saw these words on a church sign: Pray for a good harvest, but keep on hoeing.

This made me think of Jesus's words in Matthew 9. Before telling His disciples to pray that laborers would be sent out, He reminded them that a good harvest was waiting but that the laborers were few (vv. 37–38).

We sometimes forget that God may want us to be part of the answer to our own prayers. We expect Him to do everything, and then we sit back and do nothing.

We ask Him to bless the work of our church but offer excuses when asked to serve. We plead for loved ones to be saved, yet never speak a word of testimony to them. We earnestly intercede for people with serious financial needs, but we won't dig deep into our own pockets even though we have the means to help them. We ask the Lord to comfort and encourage the shut-ins and lonely, but we never go out of our way to pay them a visit or send them a note of encouragement.

Yes, God wants us to bring our requests to Him, but many times He wants us to add feet to our prayers. Working often goes hand-in-hand with praying.

—*Richard DeHaan*

Prayer Tip: Go out at night, look up, and praise God for the wonderful universe He created.

THE LISTENING PRAYER

Read: Psalm 86:1-12

Teach me your way, LORD, that I may rely on your faithfulness.
—PSALM 86:11

How do you feel when you talk with someone who isn't listening to you? It can happen with a friend who has his own plans for how a conversation should go. Or it can happen when the other person simply doesn't want to hear what you have to say.

Now think about this in regard to your prayer-life. Could it be that the way we talk to God is a one-sided conversation dominated by us? Notice the observation of William Barclay in *The Plain Man's Book of Prayers*: "Prayer is not a way of making use of God; prayer is a way of offering ourselves to God in order that He should be able to make use of us. It may be that one of our great faults in prayer is that we talk too much and listen too little. When prayer is at its highest, we wait in silence for God's voice to us."

We might call this "the listening prayer," and it's a practice we need to develop. We need to find a way to get alone with God in quiet, to speak to Him in earnest, taking time to listen to the urgings of the Spirit and the instruction of His Word. We must say, "Teach me your way, LORD; that I may rely on your faithfulness" (Psalm 86:11).

Are we talking so much that we don't hear what God says? If so, we need to learn the art of the listening prayer.

—*Dave Branon*

Prayer Tip: As an experiment for a short time, make it a goal to remember to pray at least one short prayer every hour—to help with praying continually.

ꝏ

LEARN TO WAIT ON GOD

Read: Psalm 62:1-8

Yes, my soul, find rest in God; my hope comes from him. —PSALM 62:5

Cha Sa-soon, a 69-year-old Korean woman, finally received her driver's license after three years of trying to pass the written test. She wanted the license so she could take her grandchildren to the zoo.

She was persistent and patient in what is normally an instant world. When we want something and cannot get it, we often complain and demand. At other times, we give up and move on if what we want cannot be quickly gratified. *Wait* is a word we hate to hear! Yet, many times the Bible tells us that God wants us to wait on Him for the right timing.

Waiting on God means patiently looking to Him for what we need. David recognized why he had to wait on the Lord. First, his salvation came from Him (Psalm 62:1). He learned that no one else could deliver him. His only hope was in God (v. 5), for God alone hears our prayers (v. 8).

Our prayers often revolve around asking God to hurry up and bless what we want to do. What if God's answer to us is simply, "Be patient. Wait upon Me"? We can pray with David: "Listen to my voice in the morning, LORD. Each morning I bring my requests to you and wait expectantly" (Psalm 5:3 NLT). We can trust His response, even if it doesn't come in the time we expect.

—*C. P. Hia*

Prayer Tip: Search out a prayer buddy.

OUR FULL-TIME INTERCESSOR

Read: Hebrews 7:11-28

He is able to save completely those who come to God through him,
because he always lives to intercede for them. —HEBREWS 7:25

It was dawn, and I was painfully aware of being only a few weeks into widowhood. After another restless night, I felt too weary to pray for myself. "Lord," I sighed, "I need someone to pray for me right now."

Almost instantly God's Spirit comforted my distraught mind with the words of Hebrews 7:25, reminding me that Jesus was praying for me that very moment. With a wave of relief, I acknowledged Him as my lifelong intercessor. I will never forget how that bleak morning became gold-tinged with hope. Since then, I have drawn courage and strength countless times from my faithful High Priest.

Scottish minister Robert Murray McCheyne (1813–1843) testified, "If I could hear Christ praying for me in the next room, I would not fear a million enemies. Yet distance makes no difference. He is praying for me!"

We too can draw courage and strength from Jesus. He is our priestly representative before God the Father.

Are difficult circumstances creating fear in your heart? By all means, ask others to pray for you. But don't forget that you can count on the prayers of Jesus himself. By faith, think of Him as praying around the clock for you, as if He were in the next room.

—Joanie Yoder

Prayer Tip: **Create a prayer bulletin board somewhere in the house.**

FACING DANGER WITH PRAYER

Read: 2 Kings 19:1-9

Now, LORD our God, deliver us from his hand, so that all the kingdoms of the earth may know that you alone, LORD, are God. —2 KINGS 19:19

Trouble lay ahead for King Hezekiah of Judah. He had just received a menacing letter from Assyria's King Sennacherib. This marauding monarch had conquered many cities, and Jerusalem was next on his list. In his letter, Sennacherib mocked the God of Israel and threatened to destroy the holy city.

We read in 2 Kings 19 that Hezekiah went immediately up to the temple and spread the letter before the Lord. He acknowledged Him as the One who created all things (v. 15). He told Him that Sennacherib had reproached the living God (v. 16). Finally, he pleaded with God to deliver Judah so that all the nations of the world would know that He alone is God (v. 19). Hezekiah's actions said, in effect, "Look, God! Read this! I need your help. Your honor is at stake!"

What an example of faith in a real God who is present and aware of our needs! Like Hezekiah, we at times face imminent danger from someone who wants to harm us. Or it may be some other kind of menacing situation. No matter what we ultimately do, our first response should be to tell God of the danger and praise Him for His greatness. Then we can trust Him for the kind of help that brings Him glory.

—*Dave Branon*

Prayer Tip: Ask your Facebook friends to give you their prayer requests.

MORNING PRAYER

Read: Psalm 92

It is good to praise the LORD and make music to your name, O Most High,
proclaiming your love in the morning and your faithfulness at night.
—PSALM 92:1–2

When British preacher and writer John Stott turned 80, a friend penned a tribute to him that highlighted his discipline of prayer. For decades, Stott began each day with a prayer like this: "Good morning, heavenly Father. Good morning, Lord Jesus. Good morning, Holy Spirit." Stott then went on to worship each member of the Trinity individually, acknowledging and praising them for their work in the lives of believers.

Then he continued, "Father, I pray that I may live this day in Your presence and please You more and more. Lord Jesus, I pray that this day I may take up my cross and follow You. Holy Spirit, I pray that this day You will fill me with Yourself and cause Your fruit to ripen in my life: love, joy, peace, patience, kindness, goodness, faithfulness, gentleness, and self-control. Holy, blessed, and glorious Trinity, three Persons in one God, have mercy upon me. Amen."

The psalmist said that "it is good to praise the LORD . . . proclaiming [His] love in the morning" (92:1–2). So why not use John Stott's prayer of praise and petition as a pattern for yours today? It's a wonderful way to begin a conversation with God.

—*David McCasland*

Prayer Tip: Post a few prayer verse plaques or note cards around the house as reminders.

PRAY OR ACT?

Read: Acts 13:1-5

So after they had fasted and prayed, they placed their hands on them and sent them off. —ACTS 13:3

A missionary comes to your church and says he needs some short-term help. Do you pray or do you act?

The youth pastor says your church needs some new musical instruments for the youth ministry. Do you pray or do you act?

A mission needs help in a soup kitchen. Do you pray or do you act?

Prayer is one of the most powerful tools we have at our disposal. It allows us to speak to the Lord and to petition Him directly for guidance and help.

But sometimes we can be the answer to our own prayer. Those are the times when we should pray *and* act. Maybe that missionary's request can be answered by your willingness to go. Perhaps you can donate a musical instrument. Are you the person God is leading to help in that soup kitchen?

In the first century, the good news of Christ was spread by people going out and taking action. That's why their story is told in a book called the Acts of the Apostles, not the Prayers of the Apostles.

We should never downplay prayer, for it is something God commanded us to do. But let's realize that sometimes we need to back up our prayers with action.

—*Dave Branon*

Prayer Tip: Pray through your church's corporate prayer needs list (if there is no such list, suggest that one be e-mailed to the people periodically).

※

DAYS OF DOUBT

Read: Psalm 77

*I will remember the deeds of the Lord; yes, I will remember
your miracles of long ago.* —PSALM 77:11

Ronald Dunn began keeping a record of answered prayers and special blessings in a little book. However, he somehow misplaced the book for a while. Several years later, at a time when his faith was floundering, he rediscovered his prayer journal. To his surprise, he had forgotten most of the incidents he had written about.

As he was reading it, something happened. "My memory of God's faithfulness was revived, and my sagging faith began to recover," he said. "Remembering had restored my confidence in the Lord." Dunn began to encourage Christians to keep a book of remembrance, recording God's activity in their lives. "One day," he writes, "it may mean the difference between victory and defeat."

In Psalm 77, Asaph's faith was also floundering. After listing his serious doubts, he asked, "Has God forgotten to be merciful?" (v. 9). Suddenly he stopped and said: "I will remember the deeds of the Lord; yes, I will remember your miracles of long ago" (vv. 10–11). The act of remembering revived his faith. Read the rest of the psalm!

Why not create your own book of remembrance, recording God's wonderful deeds? Then read it often, especially on days of doubt.

—*Joanie Yoder*

Prayer Tip: "If any of you lacks wisdom, you should ask God, who gives generously to all without finding fault, and it will be given to you" (James 1:5).

SINGING AND PRAYER

Read: Revelation 5:1–10

The four living creatures and the twenty-four elders fell down before the Lamb. Each one had a harp and they were holding golden bowls.
—REVELATION 5:8

In our Bible study group, we were examining the first five chapters of the book of Revelation. We spent time talking about the four living creatures and the twenty-four elders who sang a new song when they heard that the Lamb was worthy to open the seven-sealed scroll (Revelation 5:9–10).

One member of our group asked, "What is the significance of the objects they held in their hands? Why a harp and a bowl?"

We learned that since Old Testament days, the harp has been an instrument of worship. Psalms were often sung to the accompaniment of a harp by choirs of priests and the congregation. The golden bowls, saucerlike pans filled with incense, sent up an aroma that was pleasing to God. The rising smoke represented prayer—the prayers of the saints rising up to the Lord.

Singing and prayer are integral parts of the Christian's worship experience, both public and private. The two are often linked in Scripture. We may have a scratchy voice or sing off-key, but through song and prayer we can express our adoration to almighty God.

What about your times alone with God and your public worship? Let them include both a harp and a bowl as you worship the Lord with songs and prayer.

—*David Egner*

Prayer Tip: Create a PowerPoint with photos of people you want to pray for. As you go through each slide and see his or her picture, you'll have a visual that will help you think about how to pray for that person.

A PRAYER JESUS
NEVER PRAYED

Read: Luke 11:1-10

*One day Jesus was praying in a certain place. When he finished, one of
his disciples said to him, "Lord, teach us to pray." —LUKE 11:1*

We usually ask an expert to give us the best advice he or she
has to offer. When we're with a successful banker, we ask how
to invest our money wisely. When the disciples needed help,
they said to Jesus, "Teach us to pray" (Luke 11:1).

Because prayer was central to Jesus's ministry, He wanted
it to be vital in theirs. So He responded by giving them what
Christians call "the Lord's Prayer." Actually, the prayer is mis-
named, for Jesus himself could not have prayed it. As the Son
of God, without sin, He could not join in the petition, "Forgive
us our sins" (v. 4). The prayer should be labeled "The Disciples' Prayer." It can serve us in the same way that an outline
serves a minister when he preaches a sermon. It guides us as
we pray.

The prayer opens with an address to God: "Father." Then
follow two major sections. First, we are to worship Him as
King and talk to Him about His kingdom (v. 2). Second, we
are to speak to the Father about our place in His family—our
need for provision, pardon, and protection (vv. 3–4).

If you need help in your prayer-life, let the pattern Jesus gave
His disciples guide you. As you follow it, you will learn what
to say when you speak to the Father and how to make your
requests.

—Haddon Robinson

———

Prayer Tip: Pray for those you know who don't know Jesus as Savior—that they will learn of Him and trust in Him.

WHO'S PRAYING?

Read: 2 Timothy 1:1-7

I thank God, whom I serve, as my ancestors did, with a clear conscience, as night and day I constantly remember you in my prayers.
—2 TIMOTHY 1:3

Jim Cymbala's daughter had been running from God for a long time. Chrissy had rebelled against her family, had left home, and was living as far from God as she could.

But one night, this teenager awoke with the distinct feeling that someone was praying for her.

And someone was. The entire congregation of the church her father pastored was talking to God about her. During their weekly prayer meeting, a member suggested they should all pray for Chrissy.

Two days later, she came home. The first question she had for her startled father was this: "Who was praying for me?" She begged forgiveness and recommitted her life to Christ.

In the apostle Paul's second letter to Timothy, he told the young first-century pastor that he was praying for him night and day (1:3). Timothy was facing some big challenges, so it must have been encouraging to know that Paul was praying specifically for him.

Are there some people we know who are in bondage to sin as Chrissy was, or who are facing a challenge as Timothy was? Are we willing to spend some concentrated time praying for them? Are we confident that God will answer?

Who's praying? We all should be.

—*Dave Branon*

Prayer Tip: "I will pray with my spirit, but I will also pray with my understanding" (1 Corinthians 14:15).

HELP NEEDED

Read: Hebrews 4:9-16

Let us then approach God's throne of grace with confidence, so that we may receive mercy and find grace to help us in our time of need.
—HEBREWS 4:16

During World War II, the British Isles represented the last line of resistance against the sweep of Nazi oppression in Europe. Under relentless attack and in danger of collapse, however, Britain lacked the resources to see the conflict through to victory. For that reason, British Prime Minister Winston Churchill went on BBC radio and appealed to the world: "Give us the tools, and we will finish the job." He knew that without help from the outside, they could not endure the assault they were facing.

Life is like that. Often, we are inadequate for the troubles life throws at us, and we need help from outside of ourselves. As members of the body of Christ, that help can come at times from our Christian brothers and sisters (Romans 12:10–13)— and that is a wonderful thing. Ultimately, however, we seek help from our heavenly Father. The good and great news is that our God has invited us to come confidently before Him: "Let us then approach God's throne of grace with confidence, so that we may receive mercy and find grace to help us in our time of need" (Hebrews 4:16).

At such times, our greatest resource is prayer—for it brings us into the very presence of God. There we find, in His mercy and grace, the help we need.

—*Bill Crowder*

Prayer Tip: Read a book about prayer, such as Haddon Robinson's *Jesus' Blueprint for Prayer*. (Go to discoveryseries.org.)

✕

LORD, HEAR OUR PRAYER!

Read: Psalm 6

The Lord has heard my cry for mercy; the Lord accepts my prayer.
—PSALM 6:9

During every morning worship service in a small church I attended, the congregation would share prayer requests. After each one, the pastor would say, "Lord, in your mercy," and the people would respond, "Hear our prayer." One Sunday, a four-year-old boy behind me became more intense after each request, until he finally shouted out, "Hear our prayer!" The little boy probably expressed what a lot of us were feeling that morning.

As Christians, we believe that God hears us when we pray, not because we deserve it but because Christ has opened the way for us to talk directly to the Father. We often make our requests quietly and confidently, but there are times when we cannot help but cry out to God in heartbreak and anguish.

In Psalm 6 we can almost hear David's sobs as he pleads with God for mercy, help, and healing. Yet, even though he was faced with difficult people and overwhelming circumstances, David affirmed his trust in God: "The Lord has heard my weeping. The Lord has heard my cry for mercy; the Lord accepts my prayer" (vv. 8–9).

Today, in that mysterious blend of confidence and crying out, we can bring everything to our loving heavenly Father, saying, "Lord, in your mercy, hear our prayer!"

—*David McCasland*

Prayer Tip: If your church has a Facebook group or directory, try systematically praying through it.

HE ALWAYS ANSWERS

Read: Daniel 9:3-23

As soon as you began to pray, a word went out,
which I have come to tell you. —DANIEL 9:23

Daniel was determined to pray regularly, and it got him thrown into the lions' den (Daniel 6). But have you ever noticed how God answered his prayers?

In Daniel 9, we learn that Daniel had been reading Jeremiah's prophecy that the exile of the Israelites was supposed to end after 70 years. So Daniel prayed that God would not delay the end of the captivity. He confessed Israel's sin and asked for God's intervention.

Then, while Daniel was still praying, God not only sent an answer but He also sent His angel Gabriel to deliver it. Daniel said, "While I was still in prayer, Gabriel . . . came to me in swift flight" (v. 21). In other words, before Daniel had even finished his prayer, God heard it and immediately sent Gabriel with the answer (vv. 22–23).

Yet, on another occasion when Daniel prayed, Scripture tells us that the messenger God sent with the answer took three weeks to arrive (10:12–13).

We can learn important lessons from Daniel about how God answers our prayers today. Sometimes God sends the answer immediately. Sometimes the answer is delayed. Either way, He always answers.

—Dave Branon

———

Prayer Tip: Pray for your pastor and your pastor's family.

ALWAYS PRAY, AND DON'T GIVE UP

Read: Luke 18:1-8

Then Jesus told his disciples a parable to show them that they should always pray and not give up. —LUKE 18:1

Are you going through one of those times when it seems every attempt to resolve a problem is met with a new difficulty? You thank the Lord at night that it's taken care of but awake to find that something else has gone wrong and the problem remains.

During an experience like that, I was reading the gospel of Luke and was astounded by the opening words of chapter 18: "Then Jesus told his disciples a parable to show them that they should always pray and not give up" (v. 1). I had read the story of the persistent widow many times but never grasped why Jesus told it (vv. 2–8). Now I connected those opening words with the story. The lesson to His followers was very clear: Always pray, and never give up.

Prayer is not a means of coercing God to do what we want. It is a process of recognizing His power and plan for our lives. In prayer we yield our lives and circumstances to the Lord and trust Him to act in His time and in His way.

As we rely on God's grace not only for the outcome of our requests but for the process as well, we can keep coming to the Lord in prayer, trusting His wisdom and care for us.

Our Lord's encouragement to us is clear: Always pray, and don't give up!

—*David McCasland*

Prayer Tip: Make a daily appointment with God, and add it to your calendar.

HE ALREADY KNOWS

Read: Matthew 6:5-8

Do not be like [pagans], for your Father knows what you need before you ask him. —MATTHEW 6:8

A friend who is a commercial pilot told me about a flight in which he encountered a serious mechanical issue—a problem with dangerous implications. When the situation occurred, the warning lights in the cockpit informed him of the problem, and he monitored it all the way to the destination, ultimately landing safely.

Once on the ground, the pilot immediately went to the maintenance staff and reported it. To his surprise, the mechanics responded, "We already know about the problem and are ready to fix it. When you got the cockpit warning, we automatically got an electronic warning as well."

As he shared that incident, I couldn't help but compare it to Jesus's words about our heavenly Father: "Your Father knows what you need before you ask him" (Matthew 6:8). He said this in contrast to people who believe that they must "keep on babbling . . . for they think they will be heard because of their many words" (v. 7). Jesus presupposes God's knowledge of and concern for His children.

Even though God knows our needs, He still wants us to share our hearts with Him. He stands ready to hear our prayer and to repair our brokenness by His grace.

—*Bill Crowder*

Prayer Tip: Be persistent. God gives us permission to go to Him over and over with our requests.

PRAYING FRIENDS

Read: 1 Thessalonians 3:6-13

For you know very well that the day of the Lord will come like a thief in the night. —1 THESSALONIANS 5:2

I met my friend Angie for lunch after having not seen her for several months. At the end of our time together, she pulled out a piece of paper with notes from our previous get-together. It was a list of my prayer requests she had been praying for since then. She went through each one and asked if God had answered yet or if there were any updates. And then we talked about her prayer requests. How encouraging to have a praying friend!

The apostle Paul had a praying relationship with the churches he served, including the one at Thessalonica. He thanked God for the faith, love, and hope of the people (1 Thessalonians 1:2–3). He longed to see them and asked God "night and day" that he might be able to visit them again (3:10–11). He requested that the Lord would help their love "increase and overflow for each other and for everyone else" (v. 12). He also prayed that their hearts would be blameless before God (v. 13). They must have been encouraged as they read about Paul's concern and prayers for them. Paul knew too his own need for God's presence and power, and he pleaded, "Brothers and sisters, pray for us" (5:25).

Loving Father, thank you for wanting us to talk with you. Teach us all to be praying friends.

—Anne Cetas

Prayer Tip: Pray specifically for your children or grandchildren's schoolteachers.

X

TESTING GOD?

Read: Psalm 145

The Lord is near to all who call on him, to all who call on him in truth.
—PSALM 145:18

Margaret watched as her mother prayed for the help her poor family desperately needed. Despite those prayers, the family's poverty remained. Margaret concluded that prayer does no good.

Now, decades later, Margaret is an atheist. "It seemed to me that if prayer really worked," she said, "it would have much more effect." Margaret misinterpreted her mother's prayers to be a test for God.

Prayer is not a trial balloon we send up to see if God is there. It is an opportunity He has given us to communicate with Him. To use it as a test for God's existence is an insult to the One who created us.

Look at Psalm 145:18. There we read, "The Lord is near to all who call on him." For those in trouble, that promise has more value than any temporary physical help. The passage also points out that God expects something from us. When we pray, He expects us to "call on him in truth" (v. 18) and to "fear him" (v. 19).

God's existence is not being put to the test when we pray. We don't make requests of Him to see if He's real. When we pray, we are showing God that we have faith in Him and that we are willing to do what He says.

Prayer is not a test. It's an act of worship.

—Dave Branon

Prayer Tip: "Taste and see that the Lord is good; blessed is the one who takes refuge in him" (Psalm 34:8).

SCRIPTURE INDEX
OF KEY VERSES

OUR DAILY BREAD WRITERS

JAMES BANKS

Pastor of Peace Church in Durham, North Carolina, Dr. James Banks has written several books for Discovery House, including *The Lost Art of Praying Together* and *Prayers for Prodigals.*

DAVE BRANON

Senior editor with Discovery House, Dave has been involved with *Our Daily Bread* since the 1980s. He has written several books, including *Beyond the Valley* and *Stand Firm*, both DH publications.

ANNE CETAS

After becoming a Christian in her late teens, Anne was introduced to *Our Daily Bread* right away and began reading it. Now she reads it for a living as senior editor of *Our Daily Bread.*

POH FANG CHIA

Like Anne Cetas, Poh Fang trusted Jesus Christ as Savior as a teenager. She is an editor and a part of the Chinese editorial review committee serving in the Our Daily Bread Ministries Singapore office.

BILL CROWDER

A former pastor who is now senior content advisor for Our Daily Bread Ministries, Bill travels extensively as a Bible conference teacher, sharing God's truths with fellow believers in Malaysia and Singapore and other places where ODB Ministries has international offices. One of his popular DH books is *Let's Talk: Praying Your Way to a Deeper Relationship with God*.

LAWRENCE DARMANI

A noted novelist and publisher in Ghana, Lawrence is editor of *Step* magazine and CEO of Step Publishers. He and his family live in Accra, Ghana. His book *Grief Child*, earned him the Commonwealth Writers' Prize as best first book by a writer in Africa.

DENNIS DEHAAN (1932-2014)

In 1981 Dennis became the second managing editor of *Our Daily Bread*, replacing the original editor, Henry Bosch. A former pastor, he loved preaching and teaching the Word of God.

M. R. DEHAAN (1891-1965)

Dr. M. R. DeHaan founded this ministry in 1938 when his radio program went out over the air in Detroit, Michigan, and eventually Radio Bible Class was begun. Under his leadership, *Our Daily Bread* was first published in April 1956.

RICHARD DEHAAN (1923-2002)

Son of the founder of Our Daily Bread Ministries, Dr. M. R. DeHaan, Richard was responsible for the ministry's entrance into television. Under his leadership, *Day of Discovery*, the ministry's long-running TV program, made its debut in 1968.

DAVID EGNER

A retired editor for Our Daily Bread Ministries and long-time *Our Daily Bread* writer, David was also a college professor during his working career. In fact, he was a writing instructor for both Anne Cetas and Julie Ackerman Link at Cornerstone University.

DENNIS FISHER

As a research editor at Our Daily Bread Ministries, Dennis uses his theological training to guarantee biblical accuracy. Dr. Fisher is also an expert in C. S. Lewis studies.

VERNON GROUNDS (1914–2010)

A longtime college president (Denver Seminary) and board member for Our Daily Bread Ministries, Vernon's life story was told in the Discovery House book *Transformed by Love*.

C. P. HIA

Serving in the Our Daily Bread Ministries Singapore office, C. P. loves to teach the Bible. He sometimes assists with the Discovery Series Bible Studies from Our Daily Bread Ministries.

CINDY HESS KASPER

An editor for the Our Daily Bread Ministries publication *Our Daily Journey*, Cindy began writing for *Our Daily Bread* in 2006.

JULIE ACKERMAN LINK (1950–2015)

A book editor by profession, Julie wrote for *Our Daily Bread* from 2000 to 2015. Her book *Above All, Love* was published in 2008 by Discovery House. Julie passed away on April 10, 2015, after a lengthy battle with cancer.

DAVID MCCASLAND

Living in Colorado, David enjoys the beauty of God's grandeur as displayed in the Rocky Mountains. An accomplished biographer, David has written several books, including *Oswald Chambers: Abandoned to God* and *Eric Liddell: Pure Gold*.

KEILA OCHOA

From her home in Mexico, Keila assists with Media Associates International, a group that trains writers around the world to write about faith. She and her husband have two young children.

HADDON ROBINSON

Haddon has taught hundreds of young preachers the art of preaching. He is former president of Denver Seminary and served for many years as a professor at Gordon-Conwell Theological Seminary.

DAVID ROPER

David Roper lives in Idaho where he takes advantage of the natural beauty of his state. He has been writing for *Our Daily Bread* since 2000, and he has published several successful books with Discovery House, including *Teach Us to Number Our Days*.

JENNIFER BENSON SCHULDT

Chicagoan Jennifer Schuldt writes from the perspective of a mom of a growing family. She has written for *Our Daily Bread* since 2010, and she also pens articles for another Our Daily Bread Ministries publication: *Our Daily Journey*.

JOE STOWELL

As president of Cornerstone University, Joe stays connected to today's young adults in a leadership role. A popular speaker and a former pastor, Joe has written a number of books over the years, including *Strength for the Journey* and *Jesus Nation*.

HERB VANDER LUGT (1920–2006)

For many years, Herb was the research editor at this ministry, responsible for checking the biblical accuracy of the booklets that were published. A World War II veteran, Herb spent several years as a pastor before his tenure at Our Daily Bread Ministries began.

MARVIN WILLIAMS

Marvin's first foray into Our Daily Bread Ministries came as a writer for *Our Daily Journey*. In 2007, he penned his first *Our Daily Bread* devotional. Marvin is pastor of a church in Lansing, Michigan.

JOANIE YODER (1934–2004)

For 10 years, until her death in 2004, Joanie wrote for *Our Daily Bread*. In addition, she published the book *God Alone* with Discovery House.

NOTE TO THE READER

The publisher invites you to share your response to the message of this book by writing Discovery House, P.O. Box 3566, Grand Rapids, MI 49501, USA. For information about other Discovery House books, music, or DVDs, contact us at the same address or call 1-800-653-8333. Find us online at dhp.org or send e-mail to books@dhp.org.